Patricia Brattig (Ed.)

in.
femme fashion
1780 – 2004

Die Modellierung des Weiblichen in der Mode
The Modelling of the Female Form in Fashion

ARNOLDSCHE
Art Publishers

Inhaltsverzeichnis

Contents

1–3 Robe à la française
Deutschland / Germany,
ca. 1780

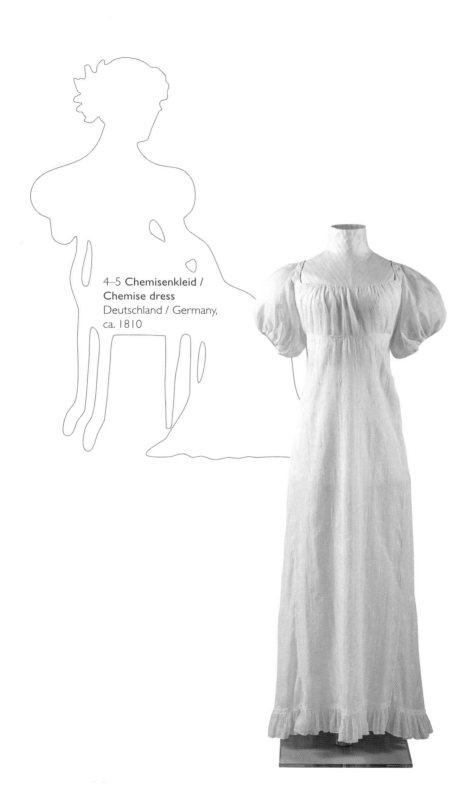

4–5 **Chemisenkleid /
Chemise dress**
Deutschland / Germany,
ca. 1810

Che soave zefiretto –
Zur Chemisenmode um 1800

Luzie Bratner

Die Gemälde der großen Porträtisten um 1800 geben die Damen der Gesellschaft in der hochaktuellen Mode wieder. Madame Julie Récamier (1777–1849), eine der berühmtesten Gesellschaftsdamen der napoleonischen Zeit, lässt sich sowohl auf dem im Louvre befindlichen Gemälde von Jacques-Louis David aus dem Jahr 1800 als auch auf dem zwei Jahre später entstandenen Porträt von François Gérard im Pariser Musée Carnavalet (Abb. 6) in einem weißen, auf den ersten Blick einfach geschnittenen Chemisenkleid darstellen. Das mit einer Schleppe bis auf den Boden herabfallende Kleid zeichnet sich durch eine hohe, unmittelbar unter die Brust verschobene Taillenlinie, ein weit ausgeschnittenes Dekolleté und sehr knappe Ärmel aus. Entscheidend für die Wirkung dieser Kleider ist neben dem Schnitt der hauchzarte Stoff. Wie dünn er ist, zeigt das Porträt von Gérard, auf dem der Knöchel des vorgestellten rechten Fußes und ein Teil der Brüste durchscheinen. Welche Art von Untergewand Madame Récamier trägt, lässt sich nicht genauer bestimmen. Als Unterwäsche sind enganliegende, hautfarbene Trikotagen überliefert, die zu einer Titulierung der Mode als „Nacktmode" führten. Das Durchschimmern des scheinbar unbekleideten Körpers unter dem leichten Chemisenkleid konnte durch seitliche Schlitze bis auf Höhe der Knie noch gesteigert werden. Bei Madame Récamier wird der Eindruck der „Nacktheit" zusätzlich durch die tatsächlich unbedeckten Schultern unterstrichen. Diese bilden, betont durch die knappen Ärmel, zudem eher eine Fortsetzung des ebenfalls sehr „nackten", tief heruntergeführten Dekolletés. Mit völlig entblößten, nur mit Diamantarmreifen geschmückten Armen und mit fleischfarbenen Seidenstrümpfen unter dem bis zum Knie gerafften Kleid war die Pariser Modekönigin Madame Tallien schon 1795 bei einem Ball in der Pariser Oper erschienen und hatte für Empörung gesorgt (Abb. 8). Auf zeitgenössischen Gemälden ist die vorgetäuschte „Nacktheit" unter den Kleidern mehr zu erahnen und niemals konkret gezeigt, wie im Gegensatz dazu auf zeitgenössischen Karikaturen. Die Transparenz der Stoffe provozierte einen regelrechten Skandal, der heftige, aber vergebliche Proteste auch von Seiten Bonapartes gegenüber der luftigen Bekleidung der sehr modebewussten Joséphine hervorrief. Es ist anzunehmen, dass diese Mode in ihrer ausgepräg-

6 François Gérard
Juliette Récamier, 1800/02

Che soave zefiretto –
The Chemise Dress around 1800

Luzie Bratner

Portraits painted around 1800 by the great exponents of that art show the ladies of society garbed at the height of fashion for their day. Madame Julie Récamier (1777–1849), one of the most celebrated holders of a salon in the Napoleonic era, is portrayed both in the Jacques-Louis David painting (in the Louvre, 1800) and the François Gérard portrait painted two years later (in the Musée Carnavalet, Paris, fig. 6) in what looks at first sight like a simply cut chemise dress. The floor-length dress with a train is notable for a high waistline pushed up to just below the bosom, a wide neckline and the briefest of sleeves. Crucial to the effect made by such dresses is, apart from the cut, the choice of gossamer-light fabric. How thin the fabric is is shown in the Gérard portrait. In it the ankle of the subject's right foot, which is placed forward, and part of the breasts are visible through the dress fabric. It is impossible to determine exactly what sort of underclothes Madame Récamier is wearing. However, knit underclothes are known to have been worn that were so close-fitting and skin-coloured that they came to be dubbed 'the nude style'. The effect created by what appeared to be an unclothed body showing through from beneath the light chemise dress could be enhanced by side slits cut as high as the knee. In the portrait of Madame Récamier the impression of 'nudity' is further underscored by her shoulders being actually bare. Moreover, emphasised as they are by the scanty sleeves, her shoulders appear more like a continuation of the very 'nude' low-cut neckline. As early as 1795, the Empress of Paris fashion, Madame Tallien, had aroused indignation by appearing at a ball in the Paris Opera with entirely exposed arms and skin-coloured silk stockings beneath a dress gathered up to the knee (fig. 8). In paintings of that period, unlike caricatures, 'nakedness' beneath clothing is merely suggested rather than actually shown. Diaphanous fabrics really caused a scandal, which called forth vehement yet futile protests even from Bonaparte at the airy cloth-ing worn by Joséphine, who was highly fashion-conscious. It is safe to assume that this fashion in its most extreme and avant-garde form was in any case only worn by ladies such as Joséphine and Madame Récamier.

testen und avantgardistischsten Form ohnehin nur von Damen wie Joséphine und Madame Récamier getragen wurde.

Auch Wilhelmine von Cotta, die Frau des Verlegers Johann Friedrich von Cotta, trägt auf dem 1802 entstandenen und in der Stuttgarter Staatsgalerie ausgestellten Porträt von Christian Gottlieb Schick ganz à la mode ein einteiliges Chemisenkleid mit Schleppe (Abb. 7). Das Gemälde entstand nach Studien Schicks zu den genannten Portraits der Madame Récamier. Im Unterschied zu den französischen Beispielen ist das Kleid allerdings weder tailliert noch gegürtet, sondern fällt fließend vom runden Ausschnitt bis zum Boden herab. Es besteht ebenfalls aus einem sehr feinen und dünnen Stoff, den der Maler in üppigen, um das Knie geführten und auf dem Boden drapierten, reich geschichteten feinen Falten wiedergibt. Frau von Cotta trägt ein dünnes Unterkleid, das am Saum mit einer Spitzenborte abschließt. Auch hier wird die Duftigkeit des Gewebes brillant wiedergegeben, so scheint das Unterkleid unter der Drapierung neben dem rechten Fuß hindurch und die Fessel zeichnet sich deutlich unter dem Untergewand ab. Die Brüste, vermeint man, schimmern hervor. Der Stoff ist aber nicht so durchsichtig, dass der Körper in solcher Konsequenz durchscheinen würde wie bei Madame Récamier. Sehr wohl aber bleibt er spürbar und unter dem Chemisenkleid gut zu erahnen.

Die Gewandung Frau von Cottas entspricht den Beschreibungen der zeitgenössischen Modejournale, wonach man in Deutschland nicht unbedingt die gewagten französischen Trikots trug. Es war vielmehr üblich, ein Unterkleid aus Taft oder Atlas zu tragen, gelegentlich sogar in anderer Farbe, was einen eigenen Effekt des Durchschimmerns ergab. Frau von Cottas Kleid ist dennoch deutlich von den „extremen" französischen Vorbildern geprägt. Das Spiel zwischen Verdecken durch den weiten Schnitt und die reichen Falten einerseits und Betonen der Körperlichkeit durch die Durchsichtigkeit des Stoffes andererseits wird schließlich in den enganliegenden Ärmeln konterkariert. Der Spitzenbesatz schafft einen fließenden Übergang von den engen Ärmeln zum unbedeckten Teil der Arme. Das Dekolleté ist jedoch

7 Christian Gottlieb Schick
Wilhelmine von Cotta, 1802

Wilhelmine von Cotta, the wife of the publisher Johann Friedrich von Cotta, is also depicted in a portrait painted by Christian Gottlieb Schick (now in the Stuttgart Staatsgalerie) entirely à la mode wearing a one-piece chemise dress with a train (fig. 7). Schick painted the portrait after studies he did from the above mentioned portraits of Madame Récamier. Unlike the French examples, however, the sitter's dress is neither nipped in at a waistline nor belted but instead falls in a fluid unbroken line from the round neckline to the floor. It, too, is made of a very fine, thin fabric, which the painter has depicted as led about the knee and draped on the floor in lavish, richly layered yet delicate folds. Frau von Cotta is wearing a thin undergarment with a lace-bordered hem. Here, too, the airiness of the fabric has been brilliantly suggested. The undergarment is visible through the draped outer garment next to the sitter's right foot and her ankle is clearly glimpsed through the petticoat. One even has the feeling that her breasts are peeping through. The fabric, however, is not so diaphanous that the body is made to show through as consistently as in the portrait of Madame Récamier. Its palpable presence, can, however, be sensed beneath the chemise dress.

Frau von Cotta's clothing matches descriptions in the fashion magazines of her day, which indicate that it was not de rigueur in Germany to wear naughty French knitted underclothes. On the contrary, the usual thing was to wear an undergarment of taffeta or satin, occasionally in a colour different to that of the outer garment to create the effect of it shimmering through the clothing worn over it. Frau von Cotta's dress is nonetheless noticeably modelled on the 'extreme' French fashions. The coquettish nod to concealment of what is underneath through the generous cut of the outer garment and rich folds, on the one hand, and the emphasis placed on the body by the transparency of the fabric on the other is ultimately counteracted by the close fit of the sleeves. The lace trimming creates a fluid transition from the tight-fitting sleeves to the part of the forearms left bare. The neckline is, on the other hand,

vergleichsweise hochgeschlossen und weit über die Brüste gezogen. Frau von Cotta trägt dazu flache Schuhe und dichte weiße Strümpfe, was allerdings durch das Porträt in der Landschaft anstelle eines Interieurs mitbedingt ist.

Die vorgestellten Gemälde ermöglichen es, die Merkmale der Chemisenkleider in einer allgemeinen Charakterisierung zusammenzufassen. Chemise, nach frz. „Hemd", bezeichnet ein hemdähnlich geschnittenes Kleid, wobei Rock und Mieder aus einem Stück genäht sein können. Unter der Brust verläuft die hochgezogene Taillenlinie, die entweder mit Hilfe einer Kordel, eines Bändchens oder durch eine einfache Naht abgetrennt ist und so eine besondere Betonung des Busens bewirkt. Das Dekolleté fällt entsprechend groß aus. Die Ärmel sind sehr kurz und können bisweilen auch ganz fehlen. Eine raffinierte Schnittführung lässt den Rücken schmal und elegant erscheinen und bietet trotz knapper Ärmel ausreichend Bewegungsfreiheit (Abb. 5, 14). Das überwiegend weiße, sehr leichte, feine und fast transparente Gewebe kommt oft ohne weitere Verzierung aus. Auf ein Oberkleid wird zeitweise völlig verzichtet, vielmehr bildet das Hemd selbst das Oberkleid. Diese Kleidung war angenehm zu tragen, zumal auf einschnürende Korsette verzichtet werden konnte. Schlichtheit und Natürlichkeit entsprachen den Idealvorstellungen der Zeit. Ebenso natürlich präsentierte sich auch die hutlose Haartracht mit kurzen Locken oder wenig gekünstelten Hochsteckfrisuren.

Vorreiter der für Directoire und Empire bezeichnenden Mode war zunächst England, wo sich die Verschiebung bzw. Aufhebung der Taille in Richtung der Brust und ein großer Ausschnitt herausgebildet hatten. In Paris wurden diese Merkmale als „mode à la grecque" in Assoziation dessen, was man für klassische griechische Gewandfiguren hielt, ab 1794/95 übernommen. In Frankreich erreichte die antikische Mode bereits 1804, dem Jahr der Kaiserkrönung Napoléons, ihren Höhepunkt und war bis etwa 1815 in ganz Europa tonangebend. Einzelne Merkmale, wie die hohe Taille, hielten sich bis etwa 1820. In Variationen blieb das Chemisenkleid aber auch in Frankreich gut ein Jahrzehnt, bis

8 „Getreue Abbildung der Madam Tallien in Paris" / 'A faithful likeness of Madame Tallien in Paris', 1797

9 Mustercoupons / Sample coupons, 1797

16

relatively high and drawn up well above the breasts. Frau von Cotta is wearing flat shoes and thick white stockings, which, of course, are necessary because she has posed outdoors and not in an indoor setting.

The paintings presented here make it possible to summarize the features of the chemise dress in a generalising characterisation. 'Chemise', meaning 'shirt' in French, denotes a dress cut similarly to a shirt, with skirt and bodice sometimes made in one piece. The waistline is high, pulled up to just below the breasts and demarcated either by a cord, a band or a simple seam to underscore the bosom. The neckline is correspondingly wide. The sleeves are very short and sometimes missing entirely. A sophisticated cut makes the back seem narrow and elegant while affording sufficient freedom of movement despite the scanty sleeves (fig. 5, 14). The fabric, mainly white, very light, fine and almost diaphanous, is often allowed to speak for itself without further trim. Outer garments were at times eschewed, being replaced by the chemise itself. This was comfortable clothing to wear, particularly since it allowed laced-in corsets to be dispensed with. The simplicity and naturalness of the chemise dress matched the ideals of the day. Hairstyles were just as natural, worn with-out hats, with the hair short and curly or worn up but without being made to look particularly artificial.

It was England that pioneered what was to become the Directoire and Empire fashions, with the waistline displaced ever further upwards towards the bosom and wider necklines. These features were adopted in Paris from 1794/95 as 'mode à la grecque' with everything then associated with classical Greek robed figures. In France the ancient Greek style was at its height by 1804, the year of Napoléon's coronation as emperor, and remained fashionable through-out Europe until about 1815. Individual features, such as the high waistline, lingered on until about 1820. Variations on the chemise dress remained en vogue in France, too, for at least a decade, until 1810, as portraits of ladies by Jean Auguste Dominique Ingres show. The generous cut, the high waistline and especially the colour white did not go out of fashion even when less delicate and increasingly glossy fabrics came into use. The clothing

1810, en vogue, wie beispielweise einige von Jean Auguste Dominique Ingres porträtierte Damen zeigen. Der weite Schnitt, die hochgezogene Taillenlinie und vor allem die weiße Farbe verloren auch bei Verwendung weniger zarter und zunehmend wieder glänzender Stoffe nicht an Aktualität. Die Gewandung der Madame Sabine Rivière auf Ingres' Gemälde (heute im Louvre) spielt 1806 noch mit der unterschiedlichen Transparenz der Stoffe, die in den ganz durchsichtigen Ärmeln einen Höhepunkt findet. Das Porträt von Cécile Bochet Madame Panckoucke (ebenfalls im Louvre) zeigt 1811 ein Kleid, das unter Beibehaltung eines beachtlichen Dekolletés vollständig in einem dichten schimmernden Satin ausgeführt ist.

Um den hauchzarten und transparenten Effekt der Chemisenkleider zu erzielen, boten sich verschiedene dünne, besonders fein gewebte und leichte leinwandbindige Stoffe an, die sonst eher für Brusttücher, Manschetten, Krägen, aber auch Taschentücher und Vorhänge Verwendung fanden. Musselin (frz. mousseline, ital. mosolino, engl. murlin; der Name leitet sich von der heute im Irak gelegenen Stadt Mossul ab) ist dabei am häufigsten anzutreffen. Der Stoff besteht meist aus Baumwolle, die sehr fein unter Verwendung gering gedrehter und nicht gesengter, also flusiger Garne, locker gewebt wird. Die Oberfläche des Musselin erscheint daher niemals vollkommen glatt, sondern eher wie mit einem leichten Flaum bedeckt. Die Luftigkeit des Halbdurchsichtigen und der weiche Fall des Stoffes haben in besonderer Weise für die Verwendung bei den Chemisenkleidern verführt. In der scheinbar kaum zu übertreffenden Feinheit des Gewebes gibt es dennoch weitere Abstufungen, so den noch feiner und lockerer gewebten Vapeur-Musselin bis hin zum allerfeinsten Zephyr, dessen Name die besondere Luftigkeit anklingen lässt. Dem dezenten Luxus der Kleider waren sowohl durch Variationen der Webart, wie beispielsweise in mousseline rayée, der ein leichtes Relief aufweist, als auch durch reiche Stickereien keine Grenzen gesetzt. Zu den Musselinstoffen zählt auch der aus Ostindien importierte Mull, der sich durch besondere Weichheit auszeichnet.

10 „Zwei nach der neuesten Französischen Mode gekleidete Damen" / 'Two ladies dressed in the newest French fashion', 1797

11 „Die neuesten Modetrachten" / 'The newest fashions in costume', 1798

worn by Madame Sabine Rivière in the Ingres painting of her (now in the Louvre) was still in 1806 playing on the varying degrees of transparency in fabrics, notably with sleeves that were entirely diaphanous. A portrait of Cécile Bochet Madame Panckoucke (also in the Louvre), painted in 1811 shows a dress made entirely of a heavy, gleaming satin although still sporting a considerable neckline.

In order to achieve the effect of ephemeral delicacy and transparency in chemise dress, various thin, especially finely tabby woven fabrics, otherwise used for kerchiefs, cuffs and collars as well as handkerchiefs and even curtains, were chosen. Mousseline or, anglicised, muslin (Fr. 'mousseline', Ital. 'mosolino', Ger. 'Musselin'; the name derives from the city of Mosul in what is now northern Iraq) is most frequently encountered. Made almost entirely of cotton yarn neither spun too much nor singed so that it was left fluffy or linty, it was loosely woven. Consequently, muslin never seems to have a perfectly smooth texture but is covered with light fluff. The airiness of this semi-transparent fabric and its soft fall were an inducement to use it for chemise dress. Although it might seem that no fabric could possibly be finer, there are in fact varying degrees of fineness, including the more delicately and loosely woven vapeur muslin and culminating in the most delicate of all, zephyr, aptly named to connote extreme airiness. No end of variations both in weaving, as in mousseline rayée, which is streaked with a slight relief texture, and embellishment with rich white-work embroidery contributed to the desired dual effect of modesty and luxury in muslin dresses. Mull, imported from the East Indies, was a type of muslin which was notable for its softness.

Ein sehr geläufiges Gewebe ist ferner der Batist (frz. batiste, ital./span. battista, engl. cambric), der, ursprünglich meist aus Leinen, vergleichsweise dichter als Musselin erscheint. Er ist durch eine sehr feine, ebenfalls halbdurchsichtige, aber dennoch feste und gleichmäßige Webart gekennzeichnet. Sein Name geht entweder auf das ostindische, Baffetas genannte Baumwollzeug, den angeblichen Erfinder Jean-Baptiste Chambray oder aber den flämischen Wortstamm für „schlagen" (batiche, frz. battre) zurück. Je nach Webart sind der leicht gewebte batiste claire, der sich hervorragend für Chemisenkleider eignete, der fester geschlagene demi claire oder moyenne und der dicht gewebte batiste hollandée zu unterscheiden. Noch feiner und leichter als Batist ist wiederum nach dem damaligen Sprachgebrauch der Linon (frz. linon, engl. lawn) oder Linonbatist, der mit viel dünneren Fäden derartig locker gewebt ist, dass er schon fast an einen Schleier erinnert. Er war nicht nur ungemustert, sondern auch wie Musselin getüpfelt oder gestreift beliebt. Als Baumwollgewebe bot sich auch Organdy an (frz. organdie, engl. book muslin), das mit ebenso feinem, aber stärker gedrehtem Faden dichter als Musselin gewebt ist und dadurch eine gewisse Steifheit besitzt, gegenüber Batist aber größere Leichtigkeit aufweist. Das Wetteifern um besonders zarte Stoffe ging soweit, dass Musselin sogar durch den netzartigen Baumwoll- oder Seiden-Tüll ersetzt wurde, der nach der gleichnamigen Stadt in Frankreich benannt ist und der einen nicht mehr zu überbietenden durchsichtigen Effekt liefert. Das Streben nach Luftigkeit und Transparenz brachte Kleider mit einem Stoffgewicht von nur 250 Gramm hervor.

12 Merveilleuse
Ende 18. Jahrhundert /
Late 18th century

Der überwiegende Bedarf an luxuriösen Stoffen konnte in Frankreich, vor allem der Picardie und Flandern gedeckt werden. Napoléon ging zeitweise allerdings soweit, die Einfuhr des indischen Musselins und auch englischer Stoffe zu verbieten, um die heimische Produktion zu fördern. Da die Stoffe extrem dünn waren, konnten sie kaum für Wärme sorgen. Außerdem verzichtete man auf einen Mantel, der durch Schals, bevorzugt kostbare Kaschmirschals, ersetzt wurde, wie dies auch auf den Porträts von Madame Récamier und Frau von Cotta zu sehen ist. Dies führte dazu, dass viele Damen sich schwere Ver-

13 „Eine Dame in neuester Modetracht" / 'A lady wearing the newest fashion in costume', 1800

Another widely used fabric was batiste or cambric (Fr. 'batiste', Ital./Span. 'battista', Ger. 'Batist'). Originally made with a high linen content, it looks thicker and feels stiffer than muslin. It is notable for a very fine, also semi-transparent yet firm and even weave. Its name derives either from an Eastindian cotton cloth called baffetas or from its alleged inventor, Jean-Baptiste Chambray, or the Flemish root ('batiche') of the French word 'battre', meaning 'to beat'. Three basic types of batiste are distinguished by weave: batiste claire, so lightly woven that it was ideally suited to the making of chemise dresses, the more firmly textured demi claire or moyenne and the densely woven batiste hollandée. Finer and lighter than batiste according to linguistic usage of the period was lawn (Fr. 'linon', Ger. 'Linon'), or linen lawn, woven so loosely of much thinner thread that it feels almost like a veil. It was popular both unpatterned or, like muslin, dotted or striped. A cotton fabric also available then was organdy (Fr. 'organdie', Ger. 'Organdy'; Engl. also 'book-muslin' from the way it was folded when sold), which was woven from thread that was just as fine as that used for muslin but more tightly spun, resulting in fabric stiffer, although more light-weight, than batiste. The demand for delicate fabrics ultimately led to muslin even being replaced by tulle, cotton or silk net named after the city of Tulle in France and of unsurpassable translucency. The striving for airiness and translucency led to the making of clothes weighing only 250 grammes.

Most of the demand for luxury fabrics could be met by France, especially Picardy, and Flanders. Napoléon occasionally even resorted to the protectionist measure of forbidding the importation of Indian muslin as well as English fabrics to promote French production. Since all these fabrics were extremely thin, they could not provide warmth. In addition, shawls, preferably costly cashmere shawls from Kashmir, replaced cloaks, as is shown in the portraits of both Madame Récamier and Frau von Cotta. The upshot was that many ladies caught heavy colds, often followed by pneumonia, aptly apostrophised at the time as the 'muslin disease'. In their most consistently followed and typical form, these dresses were

kühlungen bis zur Lungenentzündung zuzogen, die man entsprechend dem Urheber regelrecht als „Musselinkrankheit" apostrophierte. In ihrer konsequentesten und typischsten Ausführung eigneten sich diese Kleider nur für Innenräume, was sie, neben der Verwendung der raffinierten feinen Stoffe, als ausgesprochene Luxusgewandung charakterisiert und ihnen zugleich eine besondere Intimität verleiht.

Im Museum für Angewandte Kunst Köln sind einige, wahrscheinlich deutsche Beispiele für Chemisenkleider aus der Zeit um 1810 bis 1820 zu finden (Dauerleihgaben des Kölnischen Stadtmuseums), die das Typische des Schnittes und der Silhouette anschaulich machen und erlauben, die Entwicklung der Chemisenkleider der Spätzeit in groben Zügen nachzuvollziehen. Allen Kleidern gemeinsam ist die weiße Farbe, die Fertigung aus einem Baumwollstoff, die charakteristische hohe Taillennaht und der schmale Rücken, der durch Schnürung bzw. bei dem spätesten Beispiel durch Posamenten-Knöpfe betont wird. Unterhalb der Taillennaht ist der Rücken in dichte Fältchen zusammengezogen. Ferner weisen alle Modelle leicht gebauschte Ärmel in unterschiedlicher Länge auf, die sich jeweils auf die Höhe der Taillennaht beziehen. Die Ärmel der jüngeren Kleider sind entsprechend der höheren Taillennaht wesentlich kürzer. Drei Kleider aus der Zeit um 1810 sind aus weich fließendem, durch Webtechnik in sich gemustertem und durch Stickerei verziertem Musselin gefertigt. Einmal sind es nur Tupfen, beim zweiten Kleid Tupfen im gleichmäßigen Wechsel mit Streifen, die gestickte Durchbruchtechnik imitieren (Inv.Nr. T 630, T 632) und beim dritten (Abb. 4–5, Inv.Nr. T 634) in Kettenstich gestickte Streublümchen, die mit durchbrochenem Muster in Nadelarbeit gefüllt sind. Durch die ganz Ton in Ton gehaltene Musterung erhält das Gewebe eine zarte Plastizität und seinen ausschließlichen Schmuck. Die durch eine einfache Naht gebildete Taille ist ebenso wenig akzentuiert. Die kurzen Ärmel lassen sich jeweils durch dünne Bändchen ein wenig bauschen. Alle drei Kleider besitzen ferner einen knappen Miedereinsatz in Brusthöhe. Er reicht aber nicht bis an den Rand des fast eckigen, großen Dekolletés, so dass eine reizvolle Übergangszone entsteht, die die Haut durchscheinen lässt. Die Kleider

only suitable for indoor wear. Apart from their sophistication and fineness of fabric, they were obviously luxury apparel while being indoor wear lent them an air of intimacy.

There are some chemise dresses dating from ca. 1810 to 1820 in the Museum of Applied Art Cologne (Courtesy of the Kölnisches Stadtmuseum) exemplifying the typical cut and silhouette and conveying a general idea of how the chemise later developed. All these dresses have the following features in common: they are white, made of cotton fabric, the waistline seam is characteristically high and the backs narrow, emphasised by lacing or, in the latest example, by gimp buttons. The back is gathered below the waistline seam in a flurry of little folds. Further, all models have slightly puffed sleeves varying in length, in each case related to the level of the waistline. The sleeves of the later dresses are shorter to match the higher waistline seam. Three dresses dating from ca. 1810 are made of softly flowing, patterned muslin with woven in patterns and decorated with white-work embroidery. One is merely dotted, the second boasts dots alternating uniformly with stripes imitating embroidered open-work (inv.nos. T 630, T 632) and the third (figs. 4–5, inv.no. T 634) is embroidered in chain stitch with sprays of flowerets filled out with open-work embroidery. The texturing in white lends a subtle relief to the fabric and is all the decoration a dress needs. The waistline, formed by a simple seam, is emphasised with similar reticence. The short sleeves can be puffed up a bit by means of thin drawstrings. Moreover, all three dresses possess a brief bodice insert to support the wearer's breasts. Since it does not extend to the very edge of the wide, almost square neckline, an alluring transitional zone where the skin can show through is created. These are not floor-length dresses; the low-heeled shoes worn with them are to remain visible.

reichen nicht bis zum Boden, die dazu getragenen flachen Schuhe bleiben sichtbar.

Aus sehr feinem Musselin besteht auch ein auf der gesamten vorderen Rockseite, am Saum und den Ärmeln aufwendig mit breitem Faden in Flachstickerei geziertes Chemisenkleid (Inv.Nr. T 629), das wohl in dieselbe Zeit zu datieren ist. Allerdings lässt sich hier schon beobachten, dass das Dekolleté an Freizügigkeit verliert und weiter über den Busen hochgezogen ist. Auffallend ist ferner die deutliche Reduzierung des Stoffvolumens des Rockes. Ob das Kleid einen Miedereinsatz oder eventuell ein farbiges Unterkleid besessen hat, lässt sich nicht mehr sagen, da es später ein komplett neues Futter erhielt. Ein wohl um 1815 zu datierendes Kleid besteht im Vergleich zu den Musselinkleidern aus weniger durchscheinendem Batist (ohne Inv.Nr.). Das Kleid besitzt ein großes Dekolleté, das mit Hilfe einer Zugschnur unter dem Busen ausnahmsweise auf der Vorderseite gebunden wird. Am Dekolleté wird der fast eckige Ausschnitt ebenfalls mit einer eingenähten Schnur zusammengezogen. Die Taille wird durch ein weiß besticktes, nur an vier Stellen befestigtes Leibband geziert. Auch der Saum des nun wieder bodenlangen Kleides ist mit Ornamenten in Form von Pflanzenranken und einem umlaufenden Zackenband in Platt-, Knötchen- und Schlingstich geschmückt. Im Gegensatz zu den vorher genannten Beispielen gewinnt die ornamentale Ausschmückung des Rocksaumes und die Betonung der Ärmel durch stärkere Puffung an Gewicht. Ganz dem Spätempire (um 1819) gehört das letzte Beispiel an, das durch die Verwendung eines festen, nicht mehr durchsichtigen Baumwollstoffes auffällt (Abb. 14, Inv.Nr. T 440). Die Ärmel sind sehr aufwendig gearbeitet und weisen auf eine zunehmende Verbreiterung der Silhouette in der Schulterlinie hin. Ebenso werden das fast gerade gezogene und in die Schulterlinie übergehende Dekolleté, das gegenüber dem Rückenausschnitt weiter nach oben gezogen ist, durch Spitzenbesatz und der Saum durch kostbare Richelieustickerei abgesetzt – der Schmuck des Kleides ist somit an diesen Stellen konzentriert.

A chemise dress (inv.no. T 629) made of very fine muslin and elaborately decorated across the front, at the hemline and the sleeves with coarse thread in crewel stitch, probably also dates from the same period. However, here it is already apparent that the neckline is less daring and drawn up higher over the bosom. Further, the skirt is noticeably less voluminous. It is no longer possible to say whether this dress had a bodice insert or even a coloured petticoat since it was later completely lined. Another dress probably dating from ca. 1815 is made of batiste (no inv.no.), which is less diaphanous than muslin. This dress boasts a wide neckline, which can be drawn together at the front by a drawstring under the bosom as an exception to the rule. Almost square, the neckline can also be drawn tighter with a sewn-in cord. The waistline is encircled by a sash embroidered in white-work and fastened in only four places. The hem of this dress, which is by now again floor-length, is decorated with vegetal tendrils and trimmed all round with a scalloped band in crewel stitch, knot work and buttonhole stitch. With the decoration emphasizing the hemline and its more markedly puffed sleeves, this gown is more weighty-looking than the previously discussed examples. Our last example, entirely late Empire (ca. 1819) in style, is notable for being made of a stiff cotton fabric which is not at all transparent (fig. 14, inv.no. T 440). The sleeves are very elaborately worked and show that the silhouette is becoming increasingly broader at the shoulder line. Similarly, the neckline, which is almost straight across without any transition to the shoulder line since it is now higher at the back, is emphasised by lace trimming, corresponding to a hemline faced with costly Richelieu needlepoint lace – the decoration of this dress is concentrated in these two places.

Dass die feinen durchsichtigen Stoffe sogar noch in der Biedermeier-zeit bei einem ganz anderen Schnitt Verwendung gefunden haben, zeigt schließlich ein ganz aus Musselin geschneidertes Kleid aus der Zeit um 1829 (Abb. 15, Inv.Nr. T 8). Nur für den reich gefältelten und somit sehr weiten Rock ist der Stoff doppelt gelegt, wobei auch hier eine große Transparenz erhalten bleibt. Ferner findet sich bei dem hohen und gerade geschnittenen Dekolleté auch über dem Busen eine zweite Stofflage in einer schalartigen, in der Mitte gerafften Drapierung, die sich auch am Rückenausschnitt wiederholt. Die schmale Taille ist wieder an die anatomisch ihr entsprechende Stelle gerückt. Sie wird durch einen eingesetzten, breiten Stoffstreifen, der mit einem dichte-ren Stoff hinterlegt ist, zusätzlich hervorgehoben.

Die Kölner Modelle belegen, wie lange sich der Schnitt des Chemisen-kleides hält, nämlich gut zehn bis fünfzehn Jahre nachdem der Höhe-punkt in Frankreich erreicht war, und wie lange nicht nur dieser Typus, sondern auch die französische Mode als Vorbild wirksam geblieben ist. Zugleich zeigen sie, wie die feinen Stoffe, neben ihrer Verwendung für Unterkleider und Accessoires, den Charakter eines Kleides eigenstän-dig bestimmen können.

Ich danke Elke Beck, Elke Mürau und Katharina Sossou.

A dress from ca. 1829, made entirely of muslin (fig. 15, inv.no. T 8), shows that fine, translucent fabrics were still being used in the Biedermeier period even though the cut was entirely different by now. The fabric, although still highly transparent, has been doubled just for the richly folded and, therefore, voluminous skirt. Further, the high, straight neckline is also embellished with a second layer of fabric, draped above the bosom like a shawl and gathered at the centre and this feature is repeated at the back. The waistline is slender and has again fallen to the correct anatomical spot. It is emphasised by a broad inset of fabric backed with a stiffer material.

The Cologne models furnish proof of the longevity of the chemise dress. In Germany it lasted at least ten or fifteen years after its heyday in France. Moreover, these dresses show how long the influence of French fashions and not just this one type prevailed. At the same time they reveal how fine fabrics, used for gowns as well as underclothing and accessories, may determine the design and character of a dress.

My thanks to Elke Beck, Elke Mürau and Katharina Sossou.

27

14 Chemisenkleid /
Chemise dress
Deutschland / Germany,
ca. 1819

15 **Sommerkleid /**
Summer dress
Deutschland / Germany,
ca. 1829

16 Gesellschaftskleid mit
Keulenärmeln / Afternoon dress
with ‚leg of mutton‘ sleeves
Deutschland / Germany, ca. 1830/31

30

17 Gesellschaftskleid mit Pagodenärmeln /
Afternoon dress with ‚pagoda' sleeves
Köln / Cologne, ca. 1848/50

Vom Elefantenohr zur Tischglocke – Mode im Biedermeier

Patricia Brattig

Die Damen-Mode des 19. Jahrhunderts, insbesondere des Biedermeier, ist wechselhaft und äußerst vielseitig, geprägt von lokalen Eigenheiten, vor allem aber von internationalen Modeströmungen. Vermittelt durch zahlreiche Modejournale verbreiten sich neue modische Tendenzen in Windeseile in Europa, ja sogar nach Übersee.

Die modebewusste Dame verfolgt in den Zeitschriften anhand der prächtigen, suggestiven Kupferstiche und der minuziösen, in Einzelfällen von originalen Stoffmustern (Mustercoupons) begleiteten Beschreibungen der Stoffe und Farben sowie der unabdingbaren Accessoires aufmerksam das modische Geschehen in Paris und London, aber auch in Berlin oder Wien. Die modernste Zeitschrift ist das *Journal des Dames et des Modes* (von J. P. Lemaire, 1797 in Frankfurt am Main gegründet). Die darin publizierte Avantgarde findet oft erst mit zwei, manchmal sogar drei Jahren Verspätung ihren Niederschlag in anderen Magazinen wie der *Allgemeinen Modenzeitung* (seit 1798, von J. A. Bergk in Leipzig ediert). Einflussreich ist auch das von Friedrich Justin Bertuch in Weimar 1786 verlegte *Journal des Luxus und der Moden*, das zuletzt unter dem Titel *Journal für Literatur, Kunst, Luxus und Mode* bis 1827 erschien.

18 Costumes Parisiens /
Parisian costumes, 1819

Auch die weniger begüterten Gesellschaftsschichten haben Anteil an den Modeneuheiten, erlebt doch die Textilindustrie schon in der ersten Hälfte des 19. Jahrhunderts, insbesondere in England, durch die einsetzende Industrialisierung einen ungeheuren Aufschwung. Der Handwebstuhl wird vom mechanischen Webstuhl, der 1784–86 von Edmund Cartwright entwickelt wurde und bald die Dampfkraft als Antriebsquelle nutzt, verdrängt. 1805 erfindet Joseph-Marie Jacquard in Lyon den Muster-Webstuhl (Jacquardweberei). Die Mechanisierung des traditionellen Handwerks ist nicht mehr aufzuhalten und gipfelt im Juni 1844 im Schlesischen Weberaufstand, der blutig niedergeschlagen wurde. Die übrigen verarbeitenden Handwerke der Textilwirtschaft sind ebenfalls von der Mechanisierung direkt betroffen. Parallel zur industriellen Revolution vollzieht sich ferner der Wandel von der individuellen Auftragsarbeit, wie sie im Ancien Régime üblich war, zur

From 'Elephant Ear Sleeve' to Dinner-Bell – Fashions in the Biedermeier Era

Patricia Brattig

Ladies' fashions in the 19th century and in the Biedermeier era especially changed continually and were extremely diverse, shaped by local peculiarities but primarily by international fashion trends. Disseminated by a bevy of fashion journals, trends swept like the wind throughout Europe and even overseas.

The fashion-conscious Biedermeier lady kept up with styles in Berlin and Vienna as well as Paris and London, poring over the evocative copperplate illustrations in her magazines and attentively perusing the detailed descriptions of fabrics and colours, accompanied in some cases by the original fabric patterns (sample coupons) and information on the indispensable accessories to go with the clothes. The most trendy magazine of the period available to her at home was the *Journal des Dames et des Modes* (founded by J. P. Lemaire in Frankfurt am Main in 1797). The latest fashions published in it were often echoed in other German-language fashion journals, such as the *Allgemeine Modenzeitung* (from 1798, published by J. A. Bergk in Leipzig), with a time lag of two, sometimes even three, years. Another influential fashion magazine was the *Journal des Luxus und der Moden* (first published by Friedrich Justin Bertuch in Weimar in 1786), which appeared as the *Journal für Literatur, Kunst, Luxus und Mode* until 1827.

Even the less affluent classes shared in the newest fashions. After all, the textile industry had undergone an enormous upturn even in the first half of the 19th century, especially in England, through the onset of industralisation. The hand-loom was soon replaced by the power-loom, invented in 1784–86 by Edmund Cartwright, which ran on steam. In 1805 Joseph-Marie Jacquard invented a loom for weaving patterns into cloth (Jacquard weaving) in Lyon. The mechanisation of what had been traditionally a handicraft was unstoppable, ultimately leading to the Silesian Weavers' Revolt in June 1844, which was quelled with great bloodshed. The other branches of the textile industry were also directly affected by industrialisation. Further, bespoke tailoring by individual commission, which was still the norm under the Ancien Régime, evolved into an economy of scale, with the mass production of clothing obeying the market laws of supply and

Angebotsproduktion von Kleidung, die bis heute weltweit bestimmend ist. Das erste große Konfektionshaus wird 1824 von Pierre Parissot in Paris eröffnet: La belle Jardinière. 1839 nimmt Valentin Manheimer in Berlin die Konfektion von Damenmänteln auf. Angeboten werden zunächst einfache, seriell zu produzierende Kleidungsstücke, die durch Heimarbeiterinnen preiswert hergestellt werden können. Die Formenvielfalt, Qualität und Eleganz der tonangebenden Mode der Oberschicht bleibt jedoch für die weniger Begüterten unerreicht. Im gewöhnlichen Alltagsleben prägt die Kleidung des Volkes das Bild der Straße. Oftmals besitzt man nur eine einzige Garnitur, wer es sich leisten kann, noch eine weitere für die Sonn- und Feiertage. Demzufolge wurde seltener gewaschen als heute, was der fehlenden Licht- und Waschechtheit der bedruckten Stoffe entgegenkam, jedoch nicht der Hygiene. Kleidung, Wäsche und Stoffe sind höchst wertvoll und werden als Objekt der Begierde sogar gestohlen. Modisches Leitbild ist die städtische, besonders die Pariser Kleidung.

Die Gewebe des Biedermeier stehen noch in der Tradition des 18. Jahr-hunderts. Neu und vielfältig sind die Farben und ihre Kombinationen sowie die Muster und Motive, die ab 1830 immer abwechslungsreicher werden. Der Vorstellungskraft sind kaum noch Grenzen gesetzt: Von geometrisch-abstrakt bis zu vegetabil-veristisch sind alle Variationen vertreten. Besonders beliebt sind im Biedermeier die dünnfädigen, farbig bedruckten Baumwollstoffe (Kattune), die durch das billige Material und dessen industrielle Verarbeitung im Preis wesentlich günstiger sind als Wolltuche oder Leinengewebe. In den 1820er Jahren sind die Farben der eleganten weiblichen Garderobe durchaus noch dem Chemisenkleid des Empire verpflichtet: Weiß sind 1822, so ver-künden es die Modejournale, die vornehmsten Ballkleider. Im Sommer trägt die Dame weiße oder Ton in Ton gehaltene, bisweilen auch weiß oder farbig bestickte Kleider aus leicht transparenten Stoffen wie Musselin, Tüll oder Batist (Abb. 15). Doch weitet sich die Palette der Farbtöne von Pastell bis hin zu leuchtenden, kräftigen Tönen all-mählich aus. Hierzu kontrastieren die farblich abstechend gewähl-ten Accessoires wie Gürtel, Tücher und Schals. Von 1828 bis 1831

19 Carl Begas
Die Familie Begas / The Begas family,
1821

demand, as it still does world-wide. The first large store selling ready-to-wear clothing was opened by Pierre Parissot in Paris in 1824: La belle Jardinière. In 1839 Valentin Manheimer began to make ready-to-wear ladies' cloaks in Berlin. The apparel first available on the market consisted in simple, reasonably priced clothes which could be made in large batches by women working at home in the cottage industry. The variety of forms, the quality and elegance distinguishing the trend-setting fashions paraded by the upper classes were, however, unavailable to the less affluent. The everyday wear of the man and woman in the street was what shaped the public image of the era. Many people only owned one outfit. Those who could afford it also had a set of best clothes for Sundays and holidays. As a result, clothing was washed less frequently than nowadays. Although this did not do much for hygiene, fabrics were thus protected from the fading which would otherwise have resulted from exposure to sunlight and frequent washing since prints were not colour-fast. Clothing, underclothes and fabrics were regarded as extremely valuable items and were so sought after they were even subject to theft. Urban, especially Parisian, clothing set the trends in fashions.

Biedermeier fabrics were still rooted in 18th century tradition. What was new, on the other hand, was the variety of colours and colour combinations as well as patterns and motifs now available, which began to proliferate from 1830. The imagination was set virtually no limits: all variations were represented, ranging from geometric abstract to veristically vegetal patterns. Cotton fabrics woven of fine yarn and printed in colours (calico and chintz) were much more inexpensive than woollen cloth or linen because they were industrially manufactured. In the 1820s the elegant lady's wardrobe was still indebted for its colours to the Empire chemise dress: as fashion journals proclaimed in 1822, white was the colour of the most elegant ball gowns. Ladies wore gowns in white or toning shades or dresses made of light-weight, transparent fabrics such as muslin, tulle or batiste decorated with white-work or even coloured embroidery

ist Grau als Kleiderfarbe sehr begehrt (Abb. 16), so dass ab 1830 sogar auf Goldschmuck verzichtet und Silberschmuck bevorzugt wird. In den 1830er Jahren sind insbesondere farbenprächtige, sowohl dezente als auch kräftig gemusterte Kleiderstoffe modisch (Abb. 22–23). Im Sommer werden leichte Baumwollstoffe in hellen Farben mit Streifen- oder Streublümchenmuster getragen. Die leichten Wollstoffe für den Winter sind vielfach gestreift. In den 1840er Jahren werden helle, zarte, aber auch changierende Farbtöne für die Ballroben bevorzugt, während die Tagesgarderobe meist eine satte und gedecktere Farbpalette in Grün, Altrosa, Blau, Violett, Braun und Schwarz aufweist (Abb. 17). Als Materialien sind für festliche Anlässe insbesondere Seidenatlas, Baumwollmusselin und Tüll, an gewöhnlichen Tagen Tuch, Kaschmir, Satin und Wollmusselin sowie Organdy und Seide beliebt. Man trägt auch verstärkt wieder schwere Stoffe wie Samt, Moiré, Damast oder Brokat.

Es ist der wohlsituierten, eleganten Dame vorbehalten, Schauplatz aller modischen Fantasien zu sein. Ihre Kleidung wird zur Inszenierung, sie repräsentiert die soziale Stellung und wirtschaftliche Macht ihres Mannes. Der Wirkungskreis der Frau ist auf ihre Rolle als Mutter und Hausherrin reduziert. Sie bleibt im öffentlichen Ansehen auf das Reich des schönen Scheins beschränkt, ist doch die einzige Kunst, die man ihr zugesteht, die der Toilette. Am Abend offenbart die Dame jene Schönheit, die sie tagsüber züchtig zu verbergen hat: ihre Haare, das Dekolleté, die Arme.

Die Kleidung ist nicht nur Ausdruck der sozialen Stellung, sondern gliedert den ganzen Tagesablauf. Man wechselt sie je nach Tageszeit und Anlass. Nach dem Aufstehen trägt man einen Morgenmantel. Die Dame, die am Vormittag nicht ausgeht, empfängt in ihrem Negligé Gäste aus dem engsten Freundeskreis. Am Nachmittag schmückt sie das Gesellschafts- oder Stadtkleid, auch einfach Nachmittagskleid genannt. Es gibt für die Promenade, den Ausritt oder die Kutschfahrt die jeweils passende Toilette. Dies gilt auch für den Abend mit Freunden zu Hause, für anspruchsvollere Diners, für das Theater oder den großen Ball.

(fig. 15). Nevertheless, the palette of colours gradually widened to include everything from pastel shades to brilliant, saturated hues. Accessories such as belts, scarves and shawls were worn in strikingly contrasing colours. Grey was the fashionable colour between 1828 and 1831 (fig. 16), so much so that from 1830 gold jewellery was eschewed in favour of silver. In the 1830s colourful fabrics which might be either reticently or vibrantly printed were fashionable (figs. 22–23). Light-weight cotton fabrics in light colours with stripes or printed with sprays of flowers were worn in summer. The woollen cloth worn in winter was light and often striped. In the 1840s light, delicate and even chambray effects or watered silk (moiré) were preferred in the ballroom whereas daywear was usally in saturated and sombre greens, dusty pink, blues, purples, browns and black (fig. 17). The fabrics worn on festive occasions were primarily satin, cotton muslin and tulle and popular materials for everyday wear were worsted, cashmere, sateen, and woollen muslin as well as organdie and silk. Heavy fabrics such as velvet, moiré (watered silk), damask and brocade were once again increasingly fashionable.

It was the prerogative of the affluent elegant lady to set the scene for all sorts of fashion fantasies. Her clothing now allowed her to stage her appearances in public to represent her husband's social status and financial prowess. Women were now restricted to the roles of wife and mother. The only impact a lady might make in public was limited to the realm of beauty and appearances and the only art she was permitted to practise was the toilette. Only in the evening might ladies flaunt the beauties they were supposed to keep modestly hidden from sight during the day: their hair, necklines and arms.

Dress was not just an expression of social status. It articulated daily living. Clothes were changed to mark the time of day and the occasion. On rising in the morning a lady donned her négligé. If she stayed at home during the morning, she wore it to receive her guests if they were close friends. In the afternoon she arrayed herself in a day dress or an afternoon dress. There was a special dress for each purpose: a walking dress, a riding habit or a costume for driving in her carriage. The costume

Durch das unbequeme, mit Fischbeinstäben, Holz oder Metall verstärkte Korsett ist es für die Dame eine Notwendigkeit, mit ihrer Wäsche zugleich die Schuhe oder Stiefeletten anzuziehen sowie ihre Frisur zu richten, da sie sich mit dem Mieder nur mühsam beugen und bewegen kann. Es ist auch zwingend erforderlich, die Unterhosen im Schritt offen zu halten, um der Dame die Erleichterung ihrer Bedürfnisse ohne fremde Hilfe zu ermöglichen. Über dem Korsett trägt sie eine feine durchsichtige Bluse, die wiederum von einer engen, leicht verstärkten und komplett gefütterten Korsage verdeckt wird. Über der Unterwäsche und den Unterröcken, die mit der Zeit immer zahlreicher und durch Polsterungen und Versteifungen immer schwerer werden, zieht sie endlich das Kleid an. An solchen Stoffmengen hat sie oft schwer zu tragen, gut 10 Kilogramm und mehr. Hinzu kommen zahllose Verzierungen, Rüschen, Bänder, Besätze, dazu noch Fransen und Perlstickereien, Spitzen und Tressen. Haltung und Gestik sind somit in feste Stützen gezwängt, die sie körperlich wie moralisch einengen. Das Korsett formt und betont nicht nur den Körper entsprechend dem gängigen Schönheitsideal, sondern wacht zudem über die Haltung und Tugend seiner Trägerin.

Über dem Kleid breitet die Dame zum Ausgehen noch den Schal oder den reich verzierten Mantel. Von besonderer Bedeutung ist im 19. Jahrhundert und auch im Biedermeier der große langrechteckige oder quadratische Kaschmirschal aus Wolle, Seide oder Halbseide, der den Mantel ersetzt (Abb. 22, 24–25). Vorbild sind die aus der feinen Wolle der Kaschmirziege gewebten orientalischen Schals, die schon vor der Französischen Revolution in Europa bekannt und seitdem als modisches Accessoire sehr begehrt sind (Abb. 6–7).

Vielfältig sind im Biedermeier die Entwürfe und Formen der Hüte, die wie der Sonnenschirm, der Fächer, die Handschuhe und vor allem der Schmuck unbedingt zum vollständigen Kostüm der Dame gehören. Getragen werden im Hause feine Hauben aus Spitze oder Tüll (Abb. 19), im Freien Kappen (Toques), ausladende Hüte mit weiten kreisrunden Krempen (Abb. 21, 22 links), die unter dem Kinn zu

20 Costumes Parisiens /
Parisian costumes, 1829

21 Costumes Parisiens /
Parisian costumes, 1830

parade continued on into the evening with informal dress worn with friends, attire for elegant dining, evening dress for the theatre and the ball gown for great occasions.

Since corsets stiffened with whalebone, wood or metal stays made it difficult for a lady to bend down or move freely, she had to put on her shoes or boots and do her hair while still in her underclothes. It was also absolutely necessary for her nickers to be slit at the crotch so she could relieve herself without help. Over her corset she wore a fine, transparent camisole which again was covered by a narrow, lightly stiffened and completely lined bodice. Finally she drew on her dress over her underclothes and petticoats, which with time grew more numerous and heavier due to padding and stiffening. The weight of all that material, often at least 10 kilograms, became more and more of a burden to be borne for fashion's sake. Not to mention all the trimmings: flounces, ribbons and facings and, as if that were not enough, fringes and beading, lace and braiding. Posture and gestures were thus firmly controlled by props and stays which exerted physical and moral constraints. The corset not only shaped and emphasised the right parts of the body to suit the prevailing ideal of beauty. It also censured the attitudes and safeguarded virtue of its wearers.

When she went out, a lady spread a shawl or a richly decorated cloak over her dress. An important article of clothing in the Biedermeier era and the 19th century in general was the large rectangular or square cashmere shawl of wool, silk or half silk which was worn instead of a coat or cloak (figs. 22, 24–25). Modelled on the fine Indian shawls woven of the delicate wool of the Kashmir goat, it was known in Europe even before the French Revolution and from then on it was coveted as a stylish accessory (figs. 6–7).

The Biedermeier era saw the flowering of all sorts of designs and types of hats and bonnets, which, like the parasol, the fan, gloves and, of course, jewellery, were a must for the completion of a lady's toilette. At home fine lace or tulle caps were worn (fig. 19) and outdoors pert little

bindende Schute (Capote) mit langem Schirm (Abb. 18, 22 Mitte, 24–25) und zum Reitkleid der aus der Herrenmode entlehnte Zylinder. Im Sommer trägt die Dame den kunstvoll, bisweilen auch mehrfarbig geflochtenen Strohhut aus Bast oder Weizenstroh (Abb. 25). Garniert werden die Hüte mit reichlich Blumen, Bändern und Schleifen, Federn und Rüschen. Zum Abend oder zu festlichen Anlässen schmückt sich die Dame mit dem Barett oder Turban, häufig auch nur mit den eigenen naturfarbenen Haaren, in aufwendigen und meisterhaften Frisuren mit hohem Variationsreichtum in der Gestaltung des symmetrisch teilenden Scheitels, der seitlichen Lockenbüschel und des hochgesteckten Haares (Abb. 20, 23). Bei Bedarf werden zusätzlich Haarteile aus echtem Haar oder aus Seide, Verzierungen wie Spitzen, Blumen und Federn eingesetzt (Abb. 21 rechts, 22 rechts, 24).

22 Costumes allemand et français / German and French costumes, 1831

Anhand einer Synopse der modischen Postulate der Journale und der erhaltenen Kleider und bildlichen Zeitzeugnisse lassen sich Ausprägung und Entwicklung der Tendenzen des weiblichen Kostüms, der „Modellierung der Weiblichkeit" im Biedermeier summarisch nachzeichnen. In seinen Anfängen ist das Kostüm der eleganten Dame zunächst noch sehr von der vorhergehenden Empire-Mode beeinflusst. Zunehmend verlieren die knöchellangen Kleider jetzt ihre Leichtigkeit und Transparenz, behalten aber ihre weiße, helle Farbigkeit (Abb. 14). Die weibliche Silhouette verbreitert sich an den Schultern, indem die Ärmel tiefer ansetzen und die Schultern überschnitten werden (Abb. 18). Die Ärmel sind am Oberarm gebauscht oder enden in langen, engen Röhren, die bis über das Handgelenk reichen. Die hohe Taillenlinie tendiert wieder leicht nach unten. Der schlanke Rock erweitert sich trichterförmig und erscheint vorne und seitlich faltenlos und glatt. Die für die Bewegungsfreiheit notwendige Weite konzentriert sich in dicht gereihten Falten am Rücken des Kleides (Abb. 14).

toques (with no brim or little brim at all), big circular broad-brimmed hats (figs. 21, 22 left), bonnets tied beneath the chin (capote) with a long brim (figs. 18, 22 centre, 24–25) or a top-hat borrowed from gentlemen's fashions to go with the riding habit. In summer ladies wore straw hats, skilfully woven of bast or wheat straw and sometimes in several colours (fig. 25). Hats were garnished with a profusion of flowers, ribbons and bows, feathers and frills. In the evening or on festive occasions ladies sported berets or turbans on their heads although many showed off their own natural hair, coiffed in elaborate and sophisticated hairstyles affording a wealth of variations on the symmetrical centre parting, curls at the sides and hair worn up (figs. 20, 23). Hair-pieces of real hair or silk and decorations such as laces, flowers and plumes were added as needed (figs. 21 right, 22 right, 24).

A synopsis of fashion dictates gleaned from journals and clothing that has been preserved as well as contemporary visual sources are aids to surveying the formation and development of fashion trends in women's clothing, 'the modelling of femininity', in the Biedermeier era. In the early days, the way an elegant lady dressed was still influenced by the Empire style of the preceding era. With time ankle-length dresses lost their lightness and transparency yet remained white or light in colour (fig. 14). The feminine silhouette broadened at shoulder-level because sleeves were set in lower, lowering the shoulderline (fig. 18). Sleeves were puffed on the upper arm or ended in long, narrow tubes extending over the wrists. Waistlines, which had been high, moved slightly down again. Skirts, which had been slim and tubular, became wider and conical, smooth and without tucks in the front and at the sides. The width needed for freedom of movement was concentrated in densely arrayed folds at the back (fig. 14).

Das Absinken der Taillenlinie wird in den frühen 1820er Jahren zu einem Leitthema der weiblichen Mode. Ab 1821/22 sitzt die Taille fast wieder an der natürlichen Stelle (Abb. 19). Dies führt zu einer völligen Veränderung der weiblichen Silhouette: Der Aufbau der Kragen- und Schulterpartie sowie der Ärmel und der Schnitt des Rockes wandeln sich. Die Silhouette des Oberkörpers wird optisch gelängt, so z.B. durch diagonal zur Taille verlaufende Verzierungen (Abb. 20). Das Dekolleté tendiert immer mehr zu einer waagerechten Linie, die von Schulter zu Schulter reicht. Die kurzen Ärmel sind stark gepufft und stellen in der Betonung der Schulterpartie ebenfalls ein besonderes Merkmal der Mode in den 1820er Jahren dar (Abb. 15). Der Rock ist nun glockig erweitert und reich verziert (Abb. 15, 20). Vor allem beim Ballkleid wird er kürzer. Er endet hier rund 20 cm über dem Boden. Am Ende der 1820er Jahre wird auch in der Tageskleidung der Knöchel gezeigt, so dass die langen Hosenbeine der Unterwäsche unter dem Rocksaum sichtbar werden.

In den 1830er Jahren betont die Linienführung den waagerechten Ausschnitt und die sehr breit erscheinenden Schultern mit den bauschigen, großen Ärmeln (Abb. 16, 22). Diese setzen nun sehr tief an den überschnittenen Schultern an und verlagern sich von der Armkugel auf den Oberarm. Die sogenannten Keulen- (à la gigot) oder Schinkenärmel tauchen erstmals um 1824/26 auf. Sie nehmen im Laufe der Zeit immer größere Ausmaße an und beherrschen ab 1830/31 die weibliche Silhouette vollkommen (Abb. 16, 21–23). Die Stoffmassen müssen nun mit eingearbeiteten, gestärkten Unterärmeln, mit wattierten Polstern, Fischbeingestellen oder sogar dem Blankscheit (Stahlstab) in Form gehalten werden. Dabei kann der Ärmel am Unterarm auch eng anliegen, während er oben als Elefantenohrärmel stark gebauscht ist (Abb. 21, 22 links).

23 Simon Meister
Die Familie Werbrun /
The Werbrun family, 1834

Dropping waistlines became the talk of feminine fashions in the early 1820s. By 1821/22 the waistline was almost back to its anatomical location (fig. 19). This led to a complete change in the feminine silhouette, with the structure of the collar and the shoulders as well as sleeves and the cut of the skirt altered. The line of the torso appeared to have been lengthened, for instance by trimming running diagonally to the waist (fig. 20). The neckline approached a straight line in the horizontal extending from shoulder to shoulder. Sleeves were short and very puffed, representing a typical feature of 1820s fashions in the way the shoulderline was emphasised (fig. 15). Skirts became more voluminous and bell-shaped as well as richly decorated (figs. 15, 20). They also became shorter, especially for ball gowns, where they were about 20 cm above the floor. By the close of the 1820s the ankle was displayed even with daytime wear so that the long-legged pantalettes worn as underclothes peeped out beneath the hemline.

In the 1830s the silhouette emphasised the horizontal neckline and the shoulders which enormous puffy sleeves already made to appear very broad (figs. 16, 22). They were set very low on the shoulderline, falling below it, and moved from the armpit to the upper arm. The sleeves famously known as 'leg of mutton' (à la gigot) first appeared around 1824/26. With time they grew so enormous that by 1830/31 they dominated the feminine silhouette (figs. 16, 21–23). Material was now so voluminous it had to be held in shape with set in starched sleeve liners, stepped padding, whalebone frames and even steel stays (Ger. 'Blankscheit'). Sleeves might be close-fitting on the forearm to contrast with the very puffy 'elephant ear' on the upper arm (figs. 21, 22 left).

Ab 1836 werden die Ärmel dann wieder kleiner und bequemer. Der Rock wird wie der Ärmel zu Beginn der 1830er Jahre weiter und fülliger (Abb. 21–23). Da er durch Futterstoffe, Steifleinen, zahlreiche Unterröcke und sogar wieder durch die Krinoline (rosshaarversteifter Unterrock) des 18. Jahrhunderts gestützt wird und reichlich Volumen erhält, verzichtet man bald ganz auf Rüschen oder aufgesetzte Volants (Abb. 16, 23). Der Knöchel ist erst 1835/36 wieder verborgen. Die Mode passt sich dem größeren Umfang von Ärmeln und Rock an und kreiert das Mantelkleid im Schnitt der Kleider selbst (Abb. 22 Mitte). Als Überkleidung dient auch der

24 Kupferstich / Copperplate engraving, 1841

Wickler (Rotonde), ein Umhang zumeist mit großem Umlegekragen oder Kapuze. Es entstehen auch taillenkurze und lange Capes sowie über der Brust gekreuzte Schals (Mantillen) und Pelerinen.

In der Damenmode der 1840er Jahre kontrastiert die schmale Büste mit den weiten, ringsum angekrausten und bodenlangen Röcken (Abb. 17, 24–25). Bis 1845 verringert sich das Volumen von Oberkörper und Ärmeln – auch das der Haarmode und Kopfbedeckungen – kontinuierlich, so dass die Silhouette der Dame durch den überdimensionierten, kuppelförmigen Rock der Form einer Tischglocke gleicht. Das verlängerte Mieder wird zunehmend enger geschnürt, um die Taille noch zarter zu modellieren. Charakteristisch für die 1840er Jahre sind ferner die schmalen, abfallenden Schultern mit den tief ansetzenden Ärmeln (Abb. 24–25). Diese bleiben ein Indikator des modischen Wandels. Bis zur Jahrhundertmitte verringert sich ihr Umfang zusehends. Ab 1845 verbreitet sich der Ärmel wieder am unteren Ende; es entsteht der sogenannte Pagoden- oder Tütenärmel (Abb. 17), der sich trichterförmig erweitert und in den noch zusätzlich mit Weißstickerei oder Spitzen verzierte Batistärmel eingesteckt werden. Diese charakteristische Ärmelform hält sich fast bis 1860.

From 1836 sleeves again became smaller and more comfortable to wear. Like sleeves, skirts became wider and more voluminous in the early 1830s (figs. 21–23). Since the skirt was now supported by linings, buckram, numerous petticoats and the 18th-century crinoline (a horse-hair petticoat stiffen the skirt) was even revived, there was soon no need for either gathers or flounces (figs. 16, 23). Ankles were not concealed again until 1835/36. Adapting to the more voluminous sleeves and skirts, fashion brought forth the redingote cut to match dresses (fig. 22 centre). Another outer garment was the rotonde, a wraparound cloak, usually with a large turned-down collar or a hood. Capes, both waist-length and long, as well as shawls crossed at the breast (mantilles) and tippets (pelerines) also came into fashion as outer garments.

Ladies' fashions of the 1840s are notable for the contrast created between narrow bodices and wide, floor-length skirts with ruffles all round (figs. 17, 24–25). Until 1845 the volume of torso and sleeves – matched by hairstyles and head-gear – continued to be reduced so that, with the disproportionately vast dome-shaped skirt, the feminine silhouette came to resemble the shape of a dinner-bell. Bodices were longer and increasingly tightly laced to nip in the waist for a more delicate look. A further feature of the 1840s was a narrow, sloping shoulderline and sleeves set in very low (figs. 24–25). These remain an indicator of change in fashion. Until mid-century sleeves continue to widen at the lower end. The 'pagoda' or 'cornet' sleeve (fig. 17) emerged, widened at the end like a funnel, embellished inset batiste sleeves decorated with whitework embroidery or lace. This characteristic sleeve shape remained fashionable almost until 1860.

Der Bekleidungsstil der Epoche zwischen dem Wiener Kongress und dem Revolutionsjahr 1848 erweist sich als äußerst detailreich, komplex und wandelbar. Die Modekupfer der Journale und die Kostüme selbst eröffnen dem Betrachter eine kaum zu überblickende Fülle an modischen Einfällen und zeittypischen Tendenzen, an überzeichnender Formgebung sowie an Kleinteiligkeit und Verspieltheit der Ausgestaltung. Das Spiel mit der Mode, den Stoffen, ihrem Zuschnitt, ihrer Drapierung und Verzierung, findet seine Fortsetzung in der zweiten Hälfte des 19. Jahrhunderts, das an ungewöhnlichen, vor allem die weibliche Silhouette überformenden, modischen Kreationen nicht minder erfindungsreich ist als die vorangegangene Epoche.

25 Kupferstich / Copperplate engraving, 1843

Clothing worn between the Congress of Vienna (1815) and the year of the German revolution (1848) was extremely ornate, sophisticated and varied. The copperplate engravings in fashion journals and the costumes themselves reveal an almost boundless wealth of fashion ideas and trends typical of the times, exaggerated silhouettes, intricate detail and a coquettish look. Playing with fashion, materials, cut, draping and decoration continued on into the latter half of the 19th century, an era which would prove no less inventive than the preceding one in producing unusual stylish creations to reshape the feminine silhouette.

**26 Gesellschaftskleid /
Afternoon dress (crinoline)**
Deutschland oder
Großbritannien / Germany or
Great Britain, ca. 1866

27 **Gesellschaftskleid /**
Afternoon dress
Großbritannien / Great Britain,
ca. 1869/70

28 **Gesellschaftskleid /
Afternoon dress,**
ca. 1872/74

29 **Gesellschaftskleid /**
Afternoon dress
Miss Williams
Großbritannien /
Great Britain, ca. 1881/82

30 Tageskleid mit „Cul de Paris" /
Day dress with 'cul de Paris' bustle,
ca. 1884/86

31 Gesellschaftskleid / Afternoon dress
Hoflieferant Schollmeyer & Böhme /
Schollmeyer & Böhme, purveyors to the
court, Magdeburg, ca. 1894/95

Unter dem Kleid sitzt immer Fleisch

Plastische Körper und formende Blicke der Kleiderreformbewegung um 1900

Elke Gaugele

Köln, Sommer 2003: lässige weite Hosen und fließende kurze Röcke, individuell gestylt mit bauchfreien Trägertops und viel sonnengebräunter Haut bewegen sich durch die City. Plakate bewerben sexy glänzende Girls in G-Strings, Spitzen-BHs und Bikinis. Die blicken lächelnd herab auf Frauen in engen, mit langen Hosen hip kombinierten Kleidern oder auf Trägerinnen wohlgeformter Brüste unter transparenten Shirts sowie auf coole blickdichte Oberteile.

Die Modegeschichte des 20. und beginnenden 21. Jahrhunderts durchzieht eine tiefgreifende Entwicklung: Weg von der Kleider-Mode hin zur Körper-Mode lautet die Parole, die die ‚nackte Wahrheit‘ des Körpers zum Sprechen bringen will. Ein zentraler Ausgangspunkt jenes Prozesses ist die Kleiderreformbewegung um 1900 mit ihren Konzeptionen des weiblichen Körpers und seiner Kleidung. Dabei markiert das Ablegen des Korsetts, von der Frauen- und Kleiderreformbewegung als Befreiung von einem „modernen Folterinstrument" propagiert, am Ende des 19. Jahrhunderts einen zentralen historischen Wendepunkt. Im „Ansturm gegen die Mode" und in der Kritik von Korsett und Mode als „brutale Gewaltmittel" und Instrumente zur Schaffung von idealen Zerrbildern entsteht um die Jahrhundertwende ein Verständnis von Kleidung, Körper, Weiblichkeit und Identität, das unser Modeverhalten bis heute grundlegend prägt.

Für viele KleidreformerInnen der Jahrhundertwende begann die Suche nach einer neuen Frauenkleidung mit einem ‚Röntgenblick‘. „Unter dem Kleid sitzt immer Fleisch", konstatierte der Mediziner Heinrich Pudor 1903. Nur der nackte Mensch sei der wahre Mensch, der möglichst natürlich zur Geltung gebracht werden solle. Forderungen zur Abschaffung des Korsetts als Verursacher von Körperdeformationen sowie zur Befreiung der Frau vom Status der ‚Modesklavin‘ wurden in Deutschland in den 1890er Jahren von MedizinerInnen, KünstlerInnen und FeministInnen der ersten Frauenbewegung laut. Heinrich Lahmann, einer der Begründer der Naturheilkunde, und der Mediziner Gustav Jäger lieferten um 1900 erste wissenschaftliche Grundlagen zur Reformierung der Frauenkleidung. Pudor erhebt den Anspruch, dass

There is always Flesh beneath the Dress

Sculptural Bodies and shaping Perceptions of the 1900 Reform Movement in Clothing

Elke Gaugele

Cologne, summer 2003: casually flapping trousers and fluid short skirts, individually styled with halter tops to reveal the navel nestling in an expanse of sun-tanned skin saunter through the inner city. Posters advertise sexy, glossy girls in thongs, lace bras and bikinis. They smile down on women in dresses worn with long pants to look hip and on girls sporting beautiful boobs under transparent shirts and cool, glance-proof tops.

Fashion history has been going through a development with far-reaching implications in the 20th and early 21st centuries: the motto is away from clothing fashions and towards body fashions. The 'naked truth' of the body is to speak for itself. An essential new departure in this process was the reform movement which took place about 1900, brought new conceptions of the female body and how it was to be clothed. Discarding the corset as propagated by the women's and clothing reform movement as liberation from a 'modern instrument of torture' marked a major historic turning point at the close of the 19th century. The 'assault on fashion' and criticism of the corset and fashion as a 'means of brute force' as instruments for creating distorted ideal images brought forth a feeling for clothing, the body, femininity and identity which has continued to shape our fashion behaviour to the present day.

For many of the clothing men and women suffragettes the search for a new type of women's clothing began with 'X-ray vision'. 'There is always flesh beneath the dress', as Heinrich Pudor, a physician, put it in 1903. The only real person was a nude person, he thought, and respect for this real person should be achieved by as natural means as possible. Demands for the abolition of the corset as the cause of bodily deformation as well as the liberation of women from the status of 'slaves to fashion' were voiced clamorously in Germany in the 1890s by both men and women physicians, artists of both sexes and suffragettes belonging to the first women's liberation movement. Heinrich Lahmann, a pioneer of natural medicine, and Gustav Jäger, a physician, provided the first scientific foundations for the reformation of women's dress about 1900. Pudor claimed that his wife was the 'first to have worn the individualist dress of the new era' in the 1890s. Using the German translation of his name (a true

seine Frau in den 1890er Jahren diejenige gewesen sei, die das „erste individuelle Kleid der neuen Zeit" getragen habe. Unter dem Pseudonym Heinrich Scham hatte Pudor bereits 1894 eine der ersten sozialphilosophischen Pamphlete zur Nacktkultur veröffentlicht und verstand daher den nackten Körper als Ausdruck von Wahrheit und Vernunft: „die Natur kennt keine Kleider (...) der Mensch (...) als organisches Wesen, als Leben, als Geschöpf hat nichts mit Kleidern zu thun". Dem bürgerlichen Emanzipations- und Authentizitätsideal folgend war nur der anatomische Körper die Repräsentationsinstanz wahrer, natürlicher Schönheit. Während Pudor annahm, dass sich die Vernunft lediglich als nackte Wahrheit einer Person offenbare, gingen andere ReformerInnen, so z.B. Anna Muthesius, von einem anthropologischen Kleidverständnis aus: „Der Mensch ist ein bekleidetes Wesen und kann nicht mehr im Naturzustande betrachtet werden; die Bekleidung ist Teil seines Selbst geworden". Demzufolge repräsentiere sich Vernunft über Kleidung, die Ergebnis menschlichen Denkens und zugleich Maßstab für menschliche Intelligenz sei.

Die zeitgenössische Mode wurde bei der Suche nach der neuen, vernünftigen Kleidung erbittert kritisiert. Die Frauenkleidung sei ein „Armutszeugnis" wetterte der Maler und Architekt Paul Schultze-Naumburg, ein „hässlicher Fleck unserer Kultur und unvereinbar mit der geistigen Aufklärung des 20. Jahrhunderts". Obwohl die Situation von Frauen damit von den KleidreformerInnen als Grundwiderspruch der Aufklärung benannt worden war, straften sie gleichzeitig jene Frauen, die ein Korsett trugen, mit Verachtung: „Wenn die Frauen auch nur eine Spur von wirklichem Geschmack in ihrer Eitelkeit hätten, so würden sie nie ein Korsett mehr ansehen". Mode sei eine „Sünde", eine aus dem „Wahnsinn Methode" machende Strategie, schimpfte Pudor, für den Kleidung das „Gefängnis des Menschen", das „Unnatürliche" und „das Leben Negierende" darstellte. Maria van de Velde, die gemeinsam mit ihrem Ehemann Henry van de Velde Kleider schuf, die auf den bedeutendsten Ausstellungen für Reformkleidung präsentiert wurden, sah Mode als „die große Verirrte, die große Schuldige an alledem, was das Jahrhundert an hässlichem aufgespeichert hat." In ihrer „Einleitung zum Album moderner, nach Künstlerentwürfen

'speaking name' for those who know Latin and German), Heinrich Scham, as his nom de plume, Pudor had published one of the first social philosophical pamphlets on nudity by 1894. He viewed the naked human body as an expression of truth and reason: 'Nature knows no clothes [...] the human being [...] as an organic entity, as life, as creature has nothing to do with clothes.' According to the bourgeois ideal of emancipation and authenticity, the anatomical body was the sole vehicle for represent-ing true natural beauty. Whereas Pudor assumed that reason was only revealed as the naked truth of a person, other men and women reform-ers, such as Anna Muthesius, had an anthropological slant on clothing: 'The human being is a clothed being and can no longer be observed in the natural state; clothing has become part of the self.' According to this view, reason was demonstrated via clothing, the fruit of human thought and even the standard for measuring human intelligence.

The search for new, rational clothing led to harsh criticism of prevailing fashions. Ladies' clothing 'attested to intellectual and spiritual incapacity' thundered the painter and architect Paul Schultze-Naumburg, an 'unsightly blemish on our culture and irreconcilable with 20th century intellectual enlightenment'. Although this meant that clothing reformers of both sexes saw a fundamental contradiction in terms between women's situation and enlightenment, they also scornfully condemned women who wore corsets: 'If women had so much as a smattering of real taste for all their vanity, they would never look at corsets again.' Fashion, they main-tained, was a 'sin', a strategy for making 'method out of madness', sniffed Pudor, for whom clothing represented 'human incarceration', 'something unnatural' and 'negation of life itself'. Maria van de Velde, who joined forces with her husband, Henry van de Velde, to create clothes which were presented to the public at the most important exhibitions mounted by the clothing reform movement, regarded fashion as 'led greatly astray, to a great extent guilty of all the ugliest things the century had accumulated'. In an 'Einleitung zum Album moderner, nach Künstlerentwürfen ausgeführter Damenkleider, ausgestellt auf der großen allgemeinen Ausstellung für das Bekleidungswesen' ['Introduction to an album of modern ladies' clothes, executed after artists' designs and shown at the great universal exhibition for clothing'] (Krefeld 1900), she

ausgeführter Damenkleider, ausgestellt auf der großen allgemeinen Ausstellung für das Bekleidungswesen" (Krefeld 1900) kritisiert sie insbesondere den schnellen Modewechsel: Geschäfte, die „mehr auf Geld und Reklame als auf Schönheit abzielten, ersannen für jede ‚Saison' neue Änderungen der Mode und zwangen Frauen und Männern ihre Gesetze auf". Die Krefelder Ausstellung, die auch Entwürfe von Alfred Mohrbutter und Margarete von Brauchitsch zeigte, wurde von Henry van de Veldes Künstlerkleidern dominiert (Abb. 32).

Während van de Velde in seinem Einführungsvortrag über „Die künstlerische Hebung der Frauentracht" Künstler als die privilegierten Macher der Reformkleidung auswies („Es liegt in der Natur der Dinge, dass die Künstler sich mit der Frauenkleidung befassen"), kritisierte Pudor an den Kleidern van de Veldes, dass er sich zu wenig um den Bau des Körpers kümmere und das Kleid wie einen Teppich behandle. Die Flächenmuster glichen Tapeten, das Kleid sei lediglich eine willkommene Gelegenheit für Flächenornamente. Indem sie das Kleid zum Kunstwerk erklärten, sicherten van de Velde wie Mohrbutter sich den Künstlerstatus, bewegten sie sich doch mit dieser Arbeit weg vom Terrain der ‚hohen' Kunst auf das der weniger angesehenen (bisweilen weiblich kodierten) angewandten Kunst.

32 Henry van de Velde
Velvet-Kleid / Velvet dress, 1904

Dass eine Verkörperung von Weiblichkeit, wie sie seit dem 14. Jahrhundert durch das Korsett formiert worden war, immense gesundheitliche Schäden verursachen konnte, darüber waren sich alle einig: von Kopfschmerzen, Hitze, Atembeklemmungen, Appetitlosigkeit, Ohnmachtsanfällen und Schäden an allen „inneren edlen Teilen" wie Herz, Lunge oder Magen bis hin zu Fehlgeburten. Während die Gegner der Reformbewegung der Auffassung waren, „der Körper der Frau hätte ohne Korsett keinen Halt" und wäre sodann eine schlaffe, formlose Masse, argumentierten die Kleidreformer gerade konträr. Das Korsett, so ihre Argumentation, mache schlaff und fett: Es verursache eine gebeugte Haltung, da das Rückgrat durch die ständige Stütze seine gerade Haltung verliere und die Muskeln erschlafften; außerdem führe es zu Fettansätzen in der unteren Hüft- und Gesäßgegend. Wenn auch mit

was especially critical of rapid changes in fashions. Business which aimed 'more at money and advertising than beauty' devised new changes in fashion for each 'season', thus imposing its laws on both women and men'. The Krefeld exhibition, where designs by Alfred Mohrbutter and Margarete von Brauchitsch were also shown, was dominated by Henry van de Velde's artists' wear (fig. 32).

In his introductory lecture on 'The artistic elevation of women's dress', van de Velde made artists out to be the privileged creators of reform clothing ('It is in the nature of things that artists should occupy themselves with ladies' clothing'). Pudor, on the other hand, was critical of van de Velde's designs because he paid too little attention to body build and treated dresses like carpets. His surface patterns looked like wallpaper, to him a dress was merely a welcome opportunity for surface decoration. By declaring the dress a work of art, both van de Velde and Mohrbutter shored up their status as artists yet, with this achievement abandoned the territory of 'high art' for the less reputable (at times coded for femininity) applied arts.

There was universal consensus on the fact that the embodiment of femininity shaped since the 14th century by the corset might cause devastating harm to ladies' health, such as headache, hot flushes, shortness of breath, loss of appetite, fainting fits and damage to 'all the noble innards', including heart, lungs and stomach, and even miscarriages. The opponents of the reform movement believed that 'a woman's body had no support without a corset' and would be a flaccid, formless mass without one. The clothing reformers, by contrast, had recourse to a diametrically opposed line of reasoning. The corset, it went, was what made bodies flaccid and flabby: it caused bent posture since the spine lost its upright carriage by being continually supported so muscles lost their tone. In addition, the corset led to adipose deposits around the lower part of the hips and the bottom. Although they had fundamentally opposing intentions, both sides operated in discourse with the image of a female body that was flaccid, voluminous and in need of its volume being subjected to a regulating regimen of moulding (fig. 33).

grundsätzlich gegensätzlichen Intentionen, operierten dennoch beide Seiten diskursiv mit dem Bild eines schlaffen, massigen, der regulativ-plastischen Formung bedürftigen weiblichen Körpers (Abb. 33).

Auch die Suche der KleidreformerInnen war die, wie es Schultze-Naumburg formuliert, nach dem „plastisch erschauten Idealbild des Körpers". Da es nicht länger die Bekleidung sein sollte, die dem weiblichen Körper die Form aufdiktiere, sondern diese fortan der soge-nannten natürlichen Form des Körpers folgen solle, stand ein „neues Begreifen des körperlichen Prinzips" im Mittelpunkt der Reformbe-strebungen. Bei einem Verständnis des Frauenkörpers als plastische Statue, die durch den (männlichen) Blick entdeckt und dabei ästhetisch geformt wird, profilierten sich Künstler als Frauen-Bildner und Prot-agonisten weiblicher Emanzipation. Impliziert war dabei oft eine feti-schistische bzw. voyeuristische Komponente: „Ihr Körper ist bestimmt durch seine Schönheit und das Begehren des Mannes zu reizen, das Fortbestehen des Menschengeschlechts hängt davon ab". Unter dem Blick des männlichen Künstlers wird der Frauenkörper zum ‚plasti-schen Material', so auch bei der von Mohrbutter 1904 in „Das Kleid der Frau" zelebrierten Gleichsetzung von Frau und Bild (Abb. 34). Pudor riet Frauen und Kostümkünstlern, es den Malern und Bildhau-ern gleich zu tun: sich ein Modell zu nehmen, um am lebenden, unbe-kleideten Körper ihre Ideen zu erproben, nur so könne individuelle und organische Kleidung geschaffen werden.

Im Kategorisierungsfieber des ausgehenden 19. Jahrhunderts reprodu-zierte Schultze-Naumburg serienweise Fotografien und Gemälde z. T. kopfloser, nackter weiblicher Körper und darunter auch Bilder por-nografischen Inhalts (vgl. Abb. 33). Um „durch immer neue Bilder zur anschaulichen Erkenntnis der wahren Form des Körpers zu erziehen und um jene plastischen Anschauungen zu erzeugen", beurteilte er die unterschiedlichen Körperpartien minutiös. So gesehen werden in seiner Schrift „Die Kultur des weiblichen Körpers als Grundlage der Frauenkleidung" nicht nur neue mediale Leitbilder von Frauenkörpern eingeführt, sondern es wird auch eine neue Sicht auf den eigenen

33 „Von den Schäden für die Fettverteilung" / 'On the harm to adipose distribution', 1910

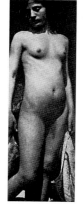

The men and women bent on reforming dress also sought, as Schultze-Naumburg put it, 'an ideal image of the body viewed sculpturally'. However, it was no longer clothing which was to impose its dictates of form on the body. On the contrary, clothing was from now on supposed to follow what was termed the natural form of the body and, in line with this perception, a 'new understanding of the body principle' was at the heart of the reform agenda. In viewing the female body as statuary in the round which was to be discovered by the (masculine) eye and aesthetically formed in this process, artists put themselves forward as sculptors of women and the vanguard of female emancipation. This often implied a fetishist or voyeur component: 'Her body is meant to arouse man's desire with its beauty; the survival of the human race depends on it.' Under the gaze of the male artist, the female body became 'modelling material', also confirmed in the equation of woman and image celebrated in Mohrbutter's 1904 'Das Kleid der Frau' ['The Lady's Dress'] (fig. 34). Pudor advised women and costume designers to do what painters and sculptors were doing: take a model in order to try out their ideas on an unclothed living body since only thus might distinctively individualised, organic clothing be created.

In line with the feverish spate of classification that broke out in the late 19th century, Schultze-Naumburg mass-produced reproductions of photographs and paintings, some of them featuring headless nude female bodies and including pictures decidedly pornographic in tone and content (cf. fig. 33). In order to 'achieve ever new images to elucidate the true form of the body and create around it sculptural ideas' he painstakingly evaluated even the most minute physical details. Viewed in this light, not only were new media images of the ideal female body introduced in his essay 'Die Kultur des weiblichen Körpers als Grundlage der Frauenkleidung' ['The Culture of the Female Body as the Basis of Women's Clothing']. A new way of viewing his own and other bodies was also included: the eye of the camera focused on and segmented all zones of the body. A catalogue of criteria for evaluating individual segments of the body was furnished in the process: 'A really exemplary profile view [...], which shows not the least trace of a bulge in the abdominal

Körper implantiert: der Kamerablick mit einer Fokussierung und Segmentierung unterschiedlichster Körperzonen. Ein Kriterienkatalog zur Beurteilung einzelner Körpersegmente wurde dabei gleich mitgeliefert: „Eine ganz mustergültige Profilansicht (…), die auch nicht die leiseste Spur einer Anschwellung in der Bauchgegend zeigt." Die flache Linie des Bauches wurde als „besonders prägnanter Ausdruck straffer und gesunder Frische" bewertet. Ein gesunder Bauch, heißt es bei Schultze-Naumburg, würde durch den „aktiven Druck der Muskeln (die sog. Bauchpresse)" flach gehalten. Diese seien „beim gesunden Menschen und zwar gleicherweise bei Mann und Weib stark genug, um den Druck der Eingeweide zu tragen, ohne sich mehr als ganz leise nach vorn auszuwölben".

34 Bucheinband von Alfred Mohrbutters „Das Kleid der Frau" / Cover of Alfred Mohrbutter 'The Lady's Dress', 1904

Leitbild der „natürlichen weiblichen Schönheit", die sich als nackte Wahrheit in Form eines straffen, muskulösen und zugleich schlanken, bewegten Körpers ästhetisch ausformulieren sollte, war die antike Statue der Venus von Milo (Abb. 35). Diese, schrieb Pudor, „hat bekanntlich niemals ein Korsett getragen; ihre Taille würde in Lebensgröße 62,5 cm betragen, sie hat Muskeln, sie hat fleißig Leibesübungen getrieben." Dass der weibliche Körper „infolge mangelnder Leibesübungen überhaupt keine Linien, sondern eine gewisse formlose Rundheit" aufweise, war für ihn ein zentrales Kriterium. Muthesius hielt dem gegenüber das Schnüren für unnötig, da Frauen schon mit einer Taille auf die Welt kämen: „Das sind die Idealfiguren nicht nur von Frauen, sondern auch von Männern."

Dem Gedanken der Aufklärung folgend ging man von einer grundsätzlichen Gleichheit des Männer- und Frauenkörpers aus (vgl. Abb. 36): „Im Aufbau der Knochen und Muskeln zeigen männliche und weibliche Körper wenig Unterschiede (…). Die Konturen des Oberkörpers von den Achseln bis zu den Hüften (…) [verlaufen] im großen und ganzen parallel." Zweigeschlechtliche Differenz würde über die „Ausnahme der Geschlechtsteile und der (inneren) Form des Beckens" definiert. Das Postulat, dass sich der schöne Körper durch Kraft und die straffe Formation seiner Muskeln selbst bilde, galt auch für die weibliche

35 Venus von Milo / Venus de Milo aus / from: Paul Schultze-Naumburg, 1910

region.' The linearity of a flat abdomen was esteemed as a 'particularly striking expression of firm, healthy freshness'. A healthy abdomen, according to Schultze-Naumburg, would be kept flat by the 'active pressure of the muscles (what is called abdominal tone)'. They (the abdominal muscles) are 'strong enough in healthy people and equally in man and woman to bear the weight of the entrails with only the merest trace of a bulge showing'.

The ideal of 'natural female beauty' which was to find aesthetic expression as the naked truth in the form of a tautly muscular, at once slender and mobile body, was the ancient statue of the Venus de Milo (fig. 35). She, wrote Pudor, 'is known never to have worn a corset; on a human scale her waist would have measured 62.5 cm; she has muscles; she did her exercises faithfully'. An important criterion for him was that the female body revealed 'no lines at all but rather a certain amorphous rotundity due to lack of regular physical exercise'. Muthesius considered lacing-in unnecessary since women had after all come into the world with a waistline: 'Those are the ideal figures, not only of women but also of men.'

In line with thoughts of enlightenment, a fundamental assumption was the corporeal equality of man and woman (cf. fig. 36): 'In the build of bone and muscle male and female bodies reveal few differences [...]. The contours of the torso from the armpits to the hips [...] [run] more or less parallel.' Gender differences were defined via the 'exception of the genitals and the (inner) form of the pelvis'. The postulate that the body beautiful formed itself through strength and the taut configuration of its muscles also applied to the female bosom: 'The most beautiful breast form is undoubtedly the perfectly uniformly rounded one which is evenly distributed across the body.' The only breasts which might rightfully claim to be beautiful were those 'which were so firm and bouncy that they might scorn the idea of being supported by artificial aids'. Such criticism of the corset was also directed at its 'wantonness', which 'more strongly than nature herself' desired, made 'breasts appear so large as if they had need of support'.

Brust: „Die schönste Form der Brüste ist zweifellos die vollkommen gleichmäßig gerundete, die ebenmäßig über den Körper verläuft." Anspruch auf Schönheit hätten lediglich solche Brüste, „die so fest und prall sind, das sie der Idee, sich von fremder Hilfe tragen zu lassen, spotten können". Die Kritik richtete sich dabei gegen die „Dirnenhaftigkeit" des Korsetts, das, „stärker als die Natur" es wolle, „die Brüste so groß erscheinen" ließe, „als ob sie der Stütze bedürften".

Die von Schultze-Naumburg formulierten Grundsätze der „neuen Frauentracht" fanden unter den meisten KleidreformerInnen Konsens: Keinerlei Art von Korsett oder Reformkorsett, BH oder weichen, losen Leibchen war beim Tragen des Kleides vorgesehen. Die genannten Stützen durften nur von den Schultern aus getragen werden und nicht unter dem Rippenkorb oder auf den Hüften Halt finden. „Gesund, praktisch, schön", lautete das Motto des 1896 gegründeten „Vereins für Verbesserung der Frauenkleidung", der ein Mitteilungsblatt mit Schnittmustern für reformierte Kleidung publizierte. Außerdem unterhielt der Verein nach ersten Ausstellungen 1897 und 1898 in Berlin seit 1899 eine ständige Präsentation von Reformkleidern, die nach folgenden Leitsätzen konzipiert waren: Vereinfachung der Unterbekleidung, Entlastung der Hüften, Erhaltung der natürlichen Form des Körpers, freie Gestaltung des Obergewandes in Anlehnung an die Mode, Verkürzung des Straßenkleides (Abb. 38–39).

Der Aspekt der Mobilität war ein zentrales Kriterium der neuen Kleidung, so dass Pudor bereits 1903 Sportbekleidung als die ideale Kleidung des modernen Menschen ansah. „Schöne Kleidung" solle, da sie elastische textile Materialien enthalte, die Körperbewegung zum Ausdruck bringen. Als schöne Bewegung galt in Opposition zur maschinellen, automatenhaften die organisch-federnde.

Kleidung repräsentiere, so Pudor, die Art „wie man sein körperliches Ego verhüllt oder verhüllend zeigt oder schmückend verhüllt oder verhüllend schmückt." In der Konzeption von Kleidung als performative Erscheinung des „körperlichen Ego" war Individualität eine elementare

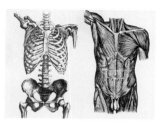

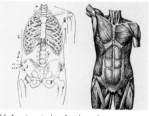

36 Anatomische Analyse /
Anatomical analysis, 1910

The basic principles of the 'new female costume' propounded by Schultze-Naumburg met with universal agreement from most men and women engaged in reforming dress: no type of corset, not even a reform corset, no brassière or soft, loose camisole was prescribed for wear beneath dresses. The underpinnings approved might only be worn from the shoulders and were not to be fastened below the rib-cage or round the hips. 'Wholesome, practical, beautiful' was the motto of the 'Verein für Verbesserung der Frauenkleidung' ['Association for the Improvement of Women's Clothing'], founded in 1896, which published a newsletter with patterns for making reformed clothing. The association mounted its first exhibitions in 1897 and 1898 and also hosted a permanent presentation of reform dress in Berlin from 1899. It was conceived on the following guidelines: simplification of underwear, relief for the hips, maintaining the natural form of the body, free design of outer garments with just a nod to prevailing fashion, raising streetwear hemlines (figs. 38–39).

The aspect of mobility was an important criterion applied to the new clothing. As a result, by 1903 Pudor for one viewed sportswear as the ideal clothing for the modern person. 'Beautiful clothing' was to express the movement of the body since it was to be made of fabrics containing elastic fibres. Beautiful movements were organic and springy, diametrically opposed to anything machine or automaton-like.

Clothing represented, thus Pudor, the way 'in which one veils one's physical ego or in veiling reveals it or in adorning veils it or veiling adorns it'. In this conception of clothing as a performative epiphenomenon of the 'physical ego', individuality was an elemental category. 'We reject all types of uniform and reform dress does not exist as far as we are concerned' was the motto of the reform association after it had been renamed in 1912 'Deutscher Verband für neue Frauenkleidung und Frauenkultur' ['German League for New Women's Clothing and Women's Culture'] in 1912. Muthesius, who took advantage of her popularity as an opera singer to disseminate ideas of clothing reform, expressed this principle as follows in 'Das Eigenkleid der Frau' ['Woman's Own Dress'] in 1903: 'The result of one's own thinking can only be dress which is adapted to

Kategorie. „Wir verwerfen jede Art von Uniform, und das Reformkleid existiert für uns nicht", war die Devise des 1912 in „Deutscher Verband für neue Frauenkleidung und Frauenkultur" umbenannten Reformvereins. Muthesius, die ihre Popularität als Opernsängerin zur Verbreitung kleidreformerischer Ideen nutzte, formulierte dies 1903 in „Das Eigenkleid der Frau" folgendermaßen: „Das Ergebnis eigenen Nachdenkens kann nur eine Bekleidung sein, die dem persönlichen Falle der Einzelnen im vollsten Sinne angepasst ist, um unsere körperliche Eigenart im guten Sinne zu steigern, unsere körperlichen Vorzüge zu heben, unsere körperlichen

37 Anna Muthesius
Haus-Kleid / Indoor dress, 1904

Nachteile zu mildern." Dabei geht sie von grundsätzlich verschiedenen Körpertypen aus, die verschiedene Anforderungen an die Bekleidung stellen. Das Eigenkleid solle „die Mängel der Natur" verdecken und die Schönheit hervorheben (Abb. 37). Die Wahrnehmung des eigenen Körpers wird dabei zur Kontrollinstanz. Über einen geschärften Blick sollten sich Frauen „genau über ihre körperlichen Vorzüge und, was noch wichtiger ist, über ihre körperlichen Fehler" bewusst werden.

Rückblickend überlappen sich die Leitbilder der KleiderformerInnen, wie das eines „plastisch erschauten Idealbilds" oder das eines „körperlichen Ego", das es zum Ausdruck zu bringen galt, mit den Körpertechniken und Blickregimes der modernen Konsumkultur. Auch hier formierte sich ein Bild des Körpers als technisch-medial gestaltbare Plastik. Korporale Identitäten und Individualität sollten über Konsumgüter und die neuen Körpertechniken wie Sport oder Diätetik hergestellt werden. Dass der „innere Körper" gepflegt werden sollte, um nach außen als performativer Ausdruck von Gesundheit in Erscheinung zu treten, ist, so der britische Soziologe Mike Featherstone 1982, ein zentrales Charakteristikum des Körpers in der Konsumkultur.

the utmost to the personal case of the individual in order to enhance our physical individuality in the good sense, to set off our physical advantages and soften our drawbacks.' She assumes fundamentally differing body types which make different demands on clothing. One's individualised dress was to conceal 'natural defects' and underscore beauty (fig. 37). One's perception of one's own body was to be the quality-control mechanism. By sharpening their eye, women were to become 'precisely aware of their physical advantages and what is even more important, their physical defects'.

Viewed in retrospect, the guidelines followed by the men and women committed to clothing reform, such as a 'sculpturally viewed ideal image' or a 'body ego' which was supposed to be expressed, coincide with the visual regime imposed by the modern consumer society. Here, too, an image of the body as sculpture to be styled by medial techniques has been formulated. Corporeal identities and individuality are supposed to be created via the new body techniques such as sport and diet control. According to the British sociologist Mike Featherstone in 1982, a main characteristic of the body in the consumer society is cultivating the 'inner body' in order to appear in public as a performative expression of good health.

Featherstone zufolge stellen Sport und Diätetik wichtige demografische Techniken dar, über die das zunehmende Lebensalter der Menschen im Industriezeitalter reguliert werden sollte. Unterzieht man die Schriften zur Reformkleidung einer näheren Betrachtung, so sind es um 1900 neben demografischen, insbesondere gender- und klassenspezifische, aber auch rassistische Argumentationsstränge, die ins Feld geführt werden. Von der „Selbstzerstörung durch die Kleidung" ist die Rede, die mit Alkoholsucht gleichgesetzt wird und eine „verheerende Wirkung auf die Zukunft unseres Geschlechts" habe. Neben der Regulierung des nationalen Volkskörpers existiert zudem die des Klassen-Körpers. Hinsichtlich ärmerer Volksschichten wurde eine „Ungewissheit und Verkommenheit des Körpers" diagnostiziert und die romantische Vorstellung vom gesunden Volkskörper aufgegeben: „Wir dürfen uns nicht mehr darauf verlassen im ‚Volke' einen Fonds von gesunden Körpern zu besitzen, der ersetzen kann, was oben leichtsinnig verdorben wird." Parallel dazu tauchen rassistische Aspekte auf. So ist des öfteren von der „nordischen Kultur" zu lesen, und Schultze-Naumburg publizierte 1928 die Schrift „Kunst und Rasse", in der „Rassen-Körper" zum Synonym für den Staatskörper wurde. Doch nicht nur als Techniken der Staats-, Klassen- und Genderkonstitution spielen Gesundheit, Sport und die Ideologie des „natürlichen Körpers" bis in den Nationalsozialismus hinein eine zentrale Rolle.

Natürlichkeit wurde, genauso wie die neuen Kleidformen, zum neuen ökonomischen Absatzmarkt. Ein Beispiel hierfür ist Helena Rubinstein, die 1892 ihre Karriere als Kosmetikerin begann und mit dem „natürlichen Gesicht" und der „sportlichen Haltung" ein Geschäftsimperium aufbaute. Natürlichkeit wurde kosmetisch durch ein raffiniertes Make-up geschaffen, das ungeschminkte Haut vortäuschte, um das Gesicht dadurch „vollkommen" zu machen. Dies entsprach Rubinsteins Devise, dass es „keine hässlichen Frauen, nur Willensschwache" gebe. Rubinsteins Salons, in denen Physiotherapeuten, Make-up-, Diät-, Haar- und Hautexperten sowie Friseure, Gymnastiklehrer und Ärzte beschäftigt waren, können getrost als Vorläufer der heutigen Fitness-studios bezeichnet werden.

Featherstone has found that sport and diet are important demographic techniques for regulating the increasing longevity enjoyed by people in the industrial age. If one subjects the writings on reform clothing to closer scrutiny, one finds that the lines of reasoning marshalled in 1900 were, apart from demographic ones, gender and class-related as well as full of racist overtones. There is talk of 'self-destruction through clothing', which is equated with alcoholism and will have a 'devastating effect on the future of our race'. Alongside the governance of the national 'folk' body there was a class body to be regulated. The poorer classes were diagnosed with 'uncertainty and physical degeneration' and the romantic idea of the healthy 'folk' body was abandoned: 'We must no longer depend on the „folk" possessing a supply of healthy bodies which can replace what is being carelessly spoilt at the top.' Racist aspects surface in parallel. 'Nordic culture' crops up frequently. In 1928 Schultze-Naumburg published 'Kunst und Rasse' ['Art and Race'], in which the 'racial body' has become synonymous with the body politic. Yet health, sports and the ideology of the 'natural body' did not just play a major role on into the National Socialist era as techniques of state, class and gender constitution.

Naturalness, like the new forms of dress, became economically important as a new market. A prime example is Helena Rubinstein, who started out as a cosmetician in 1892 and built up a business empire founded on the 'natural face' and 'athletic posture'. Naturalness was cosmetically created by means of make-up so sophisticated that it suggested unmade-up skin in order to 'perfect' the face. This matched Rubinstein's claim that there 'was no such thing as an ugly woman, just lack of will-power'. Rubinstein's salons, where physiotherapists, dieticians, trichologists, dermatologists, make-up and hairstyling experts, gymnastics instructors and physicians were employed, can certainly be described as the precursors of the present-day fitness studios.

Für die bürgerliche Frau, sagt die Kunstwissenschaftlerin Katharina Sykora 1993, war die Herstellung von Weiblichkeit eine simultane Repräsentationsarbeit von Vorzeigen und Verstecken und wurde dabei zum existenziellen Vabanque-Spiel innerhalb immer enger werdender Grenzen. Heute entlasten Starchirurgen von der anstrengenden Arbeit, den ‚natürlichen Körper' selbst zu schaffen und schneidern die jeweilige Körpermode auf den Leib. Doch ist nach wie vor das Sanduhrideal, das vom Rokoko des 18. Jahrhunderts bis zum New Look der 1950er Jahre vom Korsett geformt worden war, eine elementare Leitfigur bei der Verkörperung von ‚Weiblichkeit'.

For the middle-class woman, said the art historian Katharina Sykora in 1993, the creation of femininity was simultaneous self-staging, showing off and concealing, with the process becoming an existential gamble within increasingly narrowing limits. Nowadays star plastic surgeons relieve such women of the arduous task of creating a 'natural body' themselves and tailor bespoke body fashion right on the body. Yet the ideal of the hourglass figure, moulded from 18th century Rococo to the 1950s New Look by the corset, has remained the elemental guiding principal shaping 'femininity'.

38 **Reformkleid
(Hochzeitskleid) /**
Reform dress
(wedding dress)
Köln / Cologne, 1898

39 **Reformkleid**
(Sommerkleid) /
Reform dress
(summer dress)
Deutschland /
Germany, ca. 1909

40 **Abendkleid / Evening dress**
Großbritannien / Great Britain,
ca. 1903/07

41 Nachmittagskleid /
Afternoon dress
Berlin, 1926/27

42 **Abendkleid /
Evening dress**
Callot Sœurs, Paris,
ca. 1927/29

**43 Chiffonkleid /
Chiffon dress**
Deutschland /
Germany,
ca. 1928/30

Die Kontur der Moderne

Konstruktionen geordneter Bewegung und kontrollierter
Geschwindigkeit in der Kleidungsform der 1920er Jahre

Karen Ellwanger

Mit der Ausbreitung der klassischen Moderne in alle städtischen
Lebensbereiche hinein veränderten sich in den 1920er Jahren die
Mode und das durch sie erzeugte Körperbild grundlegend. Der sich
im ersten Drittel des 20. Jahrhunderts vollziehende Bruch mit der vorhergehenden weiblichen Modeauffassung ist als alltäglich praktizierte
Mitgestaltung innerhalb der Neuorganisation der Wahrnehmung von
Zeit und Raum zu verstehen. Diese war zur Bewältigung von maschi-
nenerzeugter Geschwindigkeit und technischer Mobilität erforderlich
geworden. Der durch die Kleidung in eine geometrisierende Kontur
gebrachte weibliche Körper (Abb. 50) repräsentiert diese Auseinandersetzung mit der Moderne und den durch sie provozierten Ängsten.
Er bringt die neue Auffassung von „Weiblichkeit" zum Ausdruck.

Seit dem späten 18. Jahrhundert hatten sich in der Kleidung erheb-
liche Unterschiede in Schnitt, Gewebe/Textur, Silhouette, Plastizität,
aber auch in Produktion und Verbreitung herausgebildet, die zugleich
die zunehmend getrennten Sphären einer Frauen- bzw. Männerkleidung kennzeichneten. In der zweiten Phase der Industrialisierung kün-
digte sich ab 1870 eine Veränderung der starren Gegenüberstellung
,männlich-weiblich' an. Da die neuen Orte bürgerlicher Öffentlichkeit
nun zumindest teilweise auch für Frauen zugänglich waren, wurden
modische Kleidungsstücke und Accessoires in den Fokus legitimierter
gesellschaftlicher Aufmerksamkeit gerückt. Aus Capes und Umschlag-
tüchern wurde der Mantel, aus der Haube ein Hut, weiche Beutel
mutierten zu straßentauglichen Handtaschen.

44 Ensemble aus Sweater und Rock /
Sweater and skirt, 1928

In ihren Grundprinzipien aber folgte die Kleidung bis zu Beginn des
20. Jahrhunderts – von Antimoden wie dem Reformkleid einmal abge-
sehen – einer etablierten Ordnung. Sie zeigt im Aufbau eine additive
Schichtung mehrerer Kleidungsstücke übereinander, denen jeweils verschiedene Bedeutung zukam. So assoziierte der amerikanische Soziologe Richard Sennett 1986 mit dem Hemd „Hygiene", mit dem Korsett
„Formung" und mit dem verheißungsvoll knisternden Seidenfutter
(„frou-frou") außerdem „Erotik". Zusätzlich betrifft diese Ordnung die
modisch wandelbaren Silhouetten, die durch Unterkonstruktion und

The Contours of Modernism

Constructs of regulated Movement and controlled Speed in 1920s Clothing Reform

Karen Ellwanger

The spread of classical Modernism throughout all domains of urban living in the 1920s brought with it fundamental change in fashion and the body image produced by fashion. The break with previous feminine notions of fashion that occurred in the first third of the 20th century entailed collusion practised daily in framing perceptual reorganisation of time and space. Such co-operative activity had become necessary for coming to terms with machine-generated pace and technical mobility. The female body, brought within a geometricising contour by clothing (fig. 50), represented this preoccupation with Modernism and the anxieties it triggered off. It expresses a new conception of 'femininity'.

Since the late 18th century considerable differences had developed in cut, weave/texture, silhouette, plasticity as well as production and distribution which at the same time characterised an increasing segregation between the spheres of women's and men's clothing. In the second phase of industrialisation a change became apparent from 1870 in the rigid dichotomy of 'masculine-feminine'. Since women now had access to the new places of bourgeois public space, at least in part, stylish clothing and accessories moved into the focus of legitimate social attention. Capes and veiling scarves turned into the coat and the hood became a hat; soft bags mutated into handbags suitable as streetwear.

In its basic principles, however, clothing – apart from such anti-fashions as the reform dress – followed an established order. It revealed an additive layering of articles of clothing, each of which had a different meaning. In 1986, for instance, the American sociologist Richard Sennett associated 'hygiene' with the blouse or shirt, 'shaping' with the corsett and, with the come-hitherish rustling of a silk lining (the sound is onomatopoeically rendered in French as 'frou-frou') 'eroticism'. In addition, this order concerns the fashionably mutable silhouettes generated by substructure and drapery such as elaborately widened, frilled or pleated textile surfaces. And, finally, mention must be made of the emphasis placed on and the sexualisation of fasteners (think of the corset-like lacing of 1880s ladies' boots), which point from visible externals to an enigmatic inner life.

Draperie erzeugt wurden, sowie die aufwendig erweiterten, gerüschten oder gefalteten textilen Oberflächen. Und schließlich ist die Betonung und Sexualisierung der Verschlüsse zu nennen (man denke an die korsettartigen Schnürungen selbst bei den Stiefeletten der 1880er Jahre), die von einem sichtbaren Äußeren auf ein geheimnisvolles Inneres verweisen.

Diese Kleidungsstruktur sowie die mit ihr verbundenen Stilmittel und Körperpraktiken sollten sich zwischen 1900 und 1930 radikal ändern. Die berühmte französische Modedesignerin Coco Chanel war maßgeblich an dieser Entwicklung beteiligt. Nicht nur ihren wegweisenden modischen Entwürfen, sondern ihrer Fähigkeit zur Verdichtung unterschiedlicher zeitgenössischer Stilanregungen, vor allem jedoch dem Mythos, den Chanel um sich selbst und ihre Produkte webte, verdankten die Frauen ein Stück neu gewonnene Bewegungsfreiheit. Mademoiselle Chanel wurde bald selbst zur Leitfigur einer aufbrechenden Zeit und verkörperte das gänzlich veränderte und moderne Lebensgefühl. Der bekleidete Frauenkörper nahm nun erheblich weniger Raum ein als im 19. Jahrhundert. Dadurch wurde er – so die amerikanische Kunsthistorikerin und Modetheoretikerin Anne Hollander – dem vom modernen Anzug geprägten Erscheinungsbild der Männer vergleichbar. Diese Reduktion ermöglichte eine größere Beweglichkeit (Abb. 44–46). Das Prinzip der Addition unterschiedlicher Kleidungsschichten mit jeweils spezifischen Bedeutungen und Funktionen wurde aufgegeben. Schon seit Ende des 19. Jahrhunderts war es zu einem damals neuen Körperideal, dem der ‚schlanken Linie‘, in Widerspruch geraten. Statt vieler Schichten besaß Frauenkleidung Mitte der 1920er Jahre im Extremfall nur noch – hier radikaler als Männerkleidung – eine zweischichtige, dünne Hülle ohne einzwängendes Korsett: die Hemdhose als Unterkleidung und das Hängerkleid (oder Rock und Jumper) als Oberkleidung. Diese Entwicklung wird in der Kostümgeschichte als „Befreiung des Körpers" beschrieben. Tatsächlich erleichterte schon die drastische Verminderung des Stoffgewichtes die Körperbewegungen. Der schnelle Wechsel der Aktionsrichtung wurde nicht länger durch eine schwerfällige Eigenbewegung der Kleidung gebremst.

45 Kostüm mit Bluse / Costume with blouse, 1928

Clothing thus structured, including the stylistic devices and body praxis linked with it, were to change radically between 1900 and 1930. Coco Chanel, the famous French fashion designer, was substantially involved in this process. Woman owed not only her revolutionary fashion creations but also her ability to condense different contemporary stylistic stimulations, yet especially the myth Chanel wove around herself and her products, a part of their recovered freedom of movement. Mademoiselle Chanel became herself soon the model of the emergent time and personified the new modern life. The clothed female body by now took up considerably less space than it had in the 19th century. Consequently, it became comparable – according to the American art historian Anne Hollander, a specialist in fashion theory – in appearance to the male body as shaped by the modern suit. Reduction of this nature made greater mobility possible (figs. 44–46). The paratactic principle of layering different articles of clothing, each with its own specific meanings and functions, was abandoned. By the end of the 19th century it had clashed with what was then a new body ideal, the 'slender figure'. Instead of so many layers, women's clothing consisted from the mid-1920s only – and in this it was more radical than menswear – in a thin wrapping made up of two layers without the constraints of a corset: the chemise or 'shimmy' as underwear and the 'flapper' tunic dress (or a sweater and skirt) as outer garments. This development is described in the history of costume as the 'liberation of the body'. The fact is that such a drastic reduction in fabric weight alone facilitated movement. Rapid change in activity directedness was no longer throttled by the movement developed independently by one's clothing.

Dennoch ist die „Befreiungs"-Metapher aus heutiger Sicht nicht mehr zu halten. Sie legt nämlich nahe, dass es unter der Kleidung einen Körper gibt, der ganz eigenen, natürlichen Gesetzen folgt, unbeeinflusst von kulturellen Bekleidungszwängen. Westliche, auf Schnittkonstruktion basierende Kleidung ist aber immer potentiell bewegungshemmend. Sie erzwingt, ermöglicht oder verhindert, unterstreicht oder verhüllt Haltung, Gestik und Bewegungsspielraum. Ferner müssen wir mit Roland Barthes annehmen, dass Kleidung den Körper erst bedeutend und kulturell sichtbar macht. Anne Hollander verdeutlichte ihrerseits am Beispiel der Aktmalerei, wie sehr die Wahrnehmung von Körperformen, -proportionen und -posen von der jeweiligen Kleidermode bestimmt ist. Insofern muss man eher von einer Kleid-Körper-Einheit sprechen und darf vermuten, dass der von dichten, textilen Hüllen ‚befreite' Körper nun selbst Kleidungsfunktionen übernahm. In den Sprachbildern der 1920er Jahre ist auch immer wieder von dem durch Gymnastik erworbenen „inneren Korsett der Muskeln" die Rede. Dass der weibliche Körper nun nicht mehr als passiv angesehen wird, sondern als straff, lokomotorisch und aktiviert (Abb. 47), entspricht einer Ideologie der Mobilisierung im Sinne einer „Durcharbeitung", wie sie für die 1920er und auch für die 1930er Jahre kennzeichnend war. „In den Tag hineinzuschlafen ist nicht länger modern", verfügt die Beilage für die „Frau in Haus, Familie und Gesellschaft", einer Tageszeitung von 1927. Nur eine „durchgearbeitete Hand" sei schön. Insgesamt ist diese Phase der Moderne weniger von einer „Befreiung" des Körpers geprägt als von einem Wandel der Bewegungsmöglichkeiten mit dem Ziel effizienter, schneller, stetiger wie auch abrupt-dynamischer (aber dadurch nicht weniger kontrollierter) Aktion.

46 Mantel mit Pelzschärpe über Rock und Sweater / Coat with fur stole over skirt and sweater, 1928

Dies wird noch deutlicher, wenn wir uns der neuen Silhouette, der Kontur im engeren Sinn, zuwenden. Sie wurde durch ein von den Schultern gerade herabfallendes Kleid oder von sich überlappenden Rock-Oberteil-Kombinationen geprägt, die nicht vorgaben, ‚natürliche' Körperformen auszudrücken. Über lange Zeit hatten eng geschnürte Taillen suggeriert, weibliche Körper seien naturgemäß in einen Ober-

Nevertheless, the 'liberation' metaphor is no longer sustainable from the present-day viewpoint. It suggests in fact that there is a body beneath clothing which follows its own natural laws, uninfluenced by the cultural constraints of clothing. Western clothing, structured on the basis of cut-out patterns, always represents a potential hindrance to movement. It compels, empowers or prevents, underscores or veils posture, gesture and scope for movement. Further, we must assume with Roland Barthes that it is clothing that makes the body a significant and culturally visible entity. Anne Hollander, for her part, used painting from the nude to demonstrate the extent to which perception of body forms, proportions and poses is determined by whatever fashion is prevailing at a given time. In this sense it would be better to speak of the unity of clothing and body and to suspect that the body 'liberated' from dense textile wrappings has itself assumed the functions of clothing. In the 1920s a recurrent metaphor refers to the 'inner corset of muscles' to be acquired by gymnastics. That the female body was then no longer viewed as passive but rather as taut, in locomotion and activated (fig. 47) corresponds to an ideology of mobilisation in the sense of 'working through' so characteristic of the 1920s and subsequently also the 1930s. 'To sleep in is no longer modern,' decreed the supplement to 'Frau in Haus, Familie und Gesellschaft' ['The Woman in the House, Family and Society'], a 1927 daily. Only a 'hand that had worked hard' was beautiful. Altogether this phase of Modernism is not so much marked by 'liberation' of the body as by a change in the possibility of movement with the aim of generating more efficient, more rapid and even abruptly dynamic (but for all that not less controlled) action.

This becomes clearer when we turn to the new silhouette, the contour in the narrower sense of the word. It was formed by dresses falling straight from the shoulder or overlapping two-piece combinations of skirts and tops which made no pretence of expressing 'natural' body forms. Nipped-in waistlines had long suggested that the female body was by nature divided into a torso and a rump strictly segregated from it. The new cut in clothes visually segmented the female body at the hip 'arbitrarily' (as contemporary critics complained), subdividing it into two

körper und in einen von diesem streng geschiedenen Unterkörper geteilt. Der neue Kleidungsschnitt segmentierte den weiblichen Körper in Hüfthöhe optisch „willkürlich" (so die zeitgenössische Kritik) und gliederte ihn in zwei rechteckige Flächen (vgl. Abb. 41). Dies sind Elemente einer konstruktivistischen Kleidung, wie sie in der Avantgarde Anfang der 1920er Jahre entwickelt wurden.

Schon die russischen Designerinnen, wie Alexandra Exter (Abb. 48) oder Warwara Stepanowa, hatten die Orientierung des modernen Bekleidungsentwurfs an Produktion und Arbeitsalltag gefordert. Stepanowa proklamierte 1923 das Primat konfektioneller Herstellung und einer damit verbundenen konstruktiven Ästhetik, die den Entstehungsprozess sichtbar werden lässt: „Wer Kleidung von heute herstellen will, muss vom Entwurfsstadium bis zur tatsächlichen Produktion eine klare Linie verfolgen. Die Nähte des Kleides und die Knöpfe müssen gut sichtbar gemacht werden. Heute gibt es keine krummen, von Hand gemachten Stiche mehr: das Nähen mit der Nähmaschine industrialisiert die Schneiderei und befreit sie von ihren Geheimnissen, wenn nicht sogar von der Faszination der Handarbeit. Die Kleidung von heute ist die Arbeitskleidung."

Im deutschen Bürgertum der 1920er Jahre fand diese programmatisch-konstruktivistische Bekleidung kaum Verbreitung. Handarbeit und Maßschneiderei spielten noch bis weit ins 20. Jahrhundert hinein eine entscheidende Rolle. Dennoch hatten diese und ähnliche Gestaltungen Einfluss auf die Ästhetik alltäglicher Kleidung. Sie folgte im weiteren Sinne konstruktivistischen Prinzipien und verwies damit nicht zufällig auf die wachsende Bedeutung von Arbeit als Anforderung an alle Bevölkerungsschichten. Die in den 1920er Jahren entwickelte Bekleidungskontur mit ihrem erweiterten Bewegungsspielraum bildete nicht zuletzt eine Voraussetzung für die Arbeit der Frauen in Angestelltenberufen mit Publikumsverkehr.

Tatsächlich scheint sich die „konstruktive Sachlichkeit" (Ellwanger 1994) in der Bekleidung Mitte und Ende der 1920er Jahre in weiten

rectangular surfaces (fig. 41). These are elements of the Constructivist clothing developed among the avant-garde of the early 1920s.

Russian designers such as Alexandra Exter (fig. 48) and Varvara Stepanova had already called for modern clothing design to be orientated towards production and the work day. In 1923 Stepanova proclaimed the primacy of ready-to-wear garment manufacture and a Constructivist aesthetic that went hand in hand with it to make the creation process visible at all stages. 'Anyone who wants to make today's clothing must pursue a clear line from the design stage to actual production. The seams and buttons of a dress must be made clearly visible. Nowadays there are no crooked stitches sewn by hand: sewing with the sewing-machine is industrialising tailoring and freeing it from its secrets, perhaps even from the fascination exerted by the handmade. Today's clothing is work clothing.'

Clothing thus programmed on Constructivist lines found little circulation among the German middle classes in the 1920s. Making garments by hand and bespoke tailoring continued to play a crucial role in womenswear until well into the 20th century. Nevertheless, Constructivist and similar conceptions of design did make an impact on the aesthetic of clothing for everyday wear. It followed Constructivist principles in the broader sense of the term, thus signifying, and not coincidentally, the growing importance of work in all classes. The clothing contour developed in the 1920s with its widened scope for movement furnished after all the precondition for women working in regular employment where they dealt with the public on a daily basis.

47 „Au loup!"
Kleiderentwürfe von Rodier /
Dress designs by Rodier, 1921

In fact, 'constructive objectivity' (Ellwanger 1994) in clothing seems to have been both widely prevalent and classless by the mid- and late 1920s. A snapshot taken by an amateur photographer in 1926 (fig. 49) shows a young woman, only recently married and before that a shop assistant, on a Sunday outing. Her clothing subdivides her body into three zones. Her legs, clad in light-coloured stockings and free to move, are what catch the eye. Then it wanders to the rump, which looks like a dark

Teilen der Bevölkerung durchgesetzt zu haben. Eine Amateurfotografie aus dem Jahre 1926 (Abb. 49) zeigt eine junge Frau, seit kurzem verheiratet und zuvor Verkäuferin, während eines Sonntagsausflugs. Ihre Bekleidung teilt den Körper in drei Zonen. Blickfang sind die hellbestrumpften, frei beweglichen Beine. Es folgt der Rumpf, der als dunkles Rechteck erscheint. Die neue Kürze des Rocksaums, der knapp unter dem Knie endet, fällt ins Auge. Der Kopf wird durch einen hellen Hut hervorgehoben und nach oben abgegrenzt. An dem sachlichen und einfachen Kleid gibt es lediglich zwei Schmuckelemente, die als kontrastreiche Betonung der Nähte gestaltet sind: Die doppelte Taschennaht rechts unterstreicht die geometrische Körperauffassung, und die Hervorhebung des Kragens betont die Möglichkeit des freien Um-Sich-Schauens.

Die Beine als lokomotorische Glieder des weiblichen Körpers wurden in Kombination mit einem geometrisierten Rumpf zum spektakulärsten Zeichen einer Kontur der Moderne. Sie verbindet die stetige Bewegung von Ort zu Ort mit der beruhigenden Statik rechter Winkel. Das durch dünne Strümpfe als ‚weiblich' gekennzeichnete Frauenbein geriet zur Metapher des Fortschritts schlechthin. Ein gewisses Unbehagen bleibt jedoch trotz aller Faszination bei den männlichen Zeitgenossen spürbar: „Mechanisch", „im Takt der Maschine" bewege sich das Frauenbein, dies entspräche der Zeit, aber man könne sich nur schwer daran wie auch an den neuen, schnellen Gang gewöhnen. Diese ambivalente Haltung wurde durch die gleichzeitige Fokussierung auf die motorischen Gliedmaßen des Oberkörpers verstärkt. Die nackten Arme wurden ebenfalls zu einem vollwertigen Darstellungsmittel (Abb. 47, 51).

Kleid und Körper, Stoff, Haut und Haare schienen in den 1920er Jahren zu einer gleichmäßig gestalteten Oberfläche zu verschmelzen. Kaum verhüllte Beine und Arme prägten das Bild der Silhouette. Neu war darüber hinaus, dass die Frisur als veränderlich, als Teil des Outfits wahrgenommen wurde – man denke an den Bubikopf und seine Varianten. Außerdem erweiterten die durch Schminke gestaltete Gesichts-

48 Kleiderentwürfe von Alexandra Exter / Dress designs by Alexandra Exter, 1923

49 Amateurfotografie / Amateur snapshot
Berlin, 1926

rectangle. The new short hemline, just below the knee, is striking. The head is emphasised and delimited at the top by a light-coloured hat. There are only two elements of decoration on this objectively simple dress which are designed to make the seams an emphatically contrasting element: the double seam on the right-hand pocket underscores the geometric conception of the body and the pronounced collar emphasizes her freedom to gaze about her as she chooses.

The legs as locomotory members of the female body have become, in combination with a geometricised rump, a Modernist contour. It links continual movement from place to place with the reassuringly static quality of the right angle. Characterised as 'feminine' by means of sheer stockings, the female leg has become the ultimate metaphor for progress. Nonetheless, a certain uneasiness is palpable among male contemporaries, for all the fascination they may have felt: the female leg moved 'mechanically', 'in time with the machine'. That matched the times but one found it difficult to become accustomed to it and even more so to the new, quick pace of walking. This ambivalent attitude was confirmed by concomitant concentration on the motoric members attached to the torso. The naked arms also became a standard focus of representation (figs. 47, 51).

Dress and body, fabric, skin and hair seem to fuse into a uniformly textured surface in the 1920s. Legs and arms that were scarcely veiled, if at all, shaped the silhouette as percept. What was new, moreover, was that hairstyles were perceived as changeable, as part of the outfit — just think of the bob and its variants. In addition, facial skin styled with make-up (fig. 52) as well as varnished nails widened the repertoire of styling resources available to broad swathes of the middle, especially urban classes. A remarkable aspect is the recourse to hygiene, a contemporary virtue: 'The hygiene of the times triumphs,' thus Paula von Reznicek in her 1928 'Ratgeber für die moderne Dame' ['Advice for the Modern Lady']. 'Fingers of any hand can be seductive if manicured – cut to look their best, superlatively groomed.' Clear-cut hemlines, the stringent demarcation of the overall clothing silhouette, incorporating armholes and neckline as well

haut (Abb. 52) und auch lackierte Nägel das Repertoire an Stilmitteln für breite bürgerliche und städtische Schichten. Bemerkenswert ist dabei der Rekurs auf die zeitgemäße Tugend der Hygiene: „Die Zeithygiene triumphiert", so Paula von Reznicek in ihrem „Ratgeber für die moderne Dame" von 1928. „Die manikürten Finger einer jeden Hand können verführerisch sein – vorteilhaft geschnitten, unerhört gepflegt." Die scharfe Linie der Rocksäume, die klare Begrenzung der gesamten Kleider-Silhouette bis hin zum Hals- und Armausschnitt sowie den Seitennähten gaben dieser Verschmelzung von Stoff und Haut Form und ordnende Struktur. Dies zeigen die typischen Tageskleider zwischen 1926 und 1928, die mit den immer gleichen, auf Amateurfotos schichtübergreifend ins Bild gesetzten, flachen Lederschuhen mit Querriemen getragen wurden. Nachmittags- und Abendkleider (Abb. 41–43, 51) hingegen durften mit fließenderen Übergängen, beweglichen Applikationen und dem Innenraum vorbehaltenen, passenden Stoffschuhen spielen.

Die Reduktion der komplexen Kleidung der Jahrhundertwende zu einer flachen, grafisch umgrenzten Straßenkleidung, die Körperbewegung zuließ, sowie die Abkehr von gefalteten, gerüschten oder stoffreich erweiterten Oberflächen eröffneten breiteren sozialen Schichten die Möglichkeit, modische Kleidung zu tragen. Die locker herabhängenden, faltenarmen Kleider ließen sich auch von Laien leicht nachschneidern. Der Zwischenraum zwischen Haut und Stoff machte analog zum Männeranzug Körper und Kleidung gegeneinander verschiebbar und distanzierbar. Die Kleidung verzichtete nun darauf, sich tief ins Fleisch einzugraben (wie in den Jahrhunderten zuvor das Mieder) und so Vorstellungen der Modellierbarkeit des weiblichen Körpers zu erzeugen.

as the side seams lent form and ordering structure to the fusion of fabric and skin. The everyday clothing typical between 1926 and 1928, which is shown in snapshots taken by amateur photographers as invariably worn with unrelentingly classless, low-heeled shoes with straps across the instep. Afternoon and evening dresses (figs. 41–43, 51), on the other hand, were permitted the play of fluid transitions, mobile appliqués and shoes in matching fabrics reserved for indoor wear.

The reduction of the complex clothing worn at the turn of the century to flat, graphically outlined streetwear permitting free movement as well as the rejection of pleated and frilled surfaces incorporating vast quantities of fabric opened up for a broader demographic segment the possibility of wearing stylish clothing. Casual dresses hanging loosely with few folds could now be easily sewn at home. The interstices between skin and fabric made, just as they did with men's suits, body and clothing movable and kept it at a remove. Clothing now eschewed biting deep into the flesh (as the bodice had done in previous centuries) to create notions of the malleability of the female body as a kneadable entity.

50 Modezeichnung von Hete Behrens / Fashion drawing by Hete Behrens Köln / Cologne, ca. 1931

At the same time, however, this arrangement, being an ensemble indicative of hard times, quickly congealed into what was recognisably a recurrent pattern. In a 1927 leader that appeared in the Ullstein press, Käthe Marcus, a Berliner, was scathing about the 'typified woman': sporting a bob, slender, short skirt. This noticeably altered, new basic form for clothing was, she stormed, the same everywhere. 'Uniformity of form' held not just for choice of shape, fabric and colour but entailed the establishment of norms governing everything worn and how it was to be worn.

Zugleich aber gefror diese Anordnung als Ensemble knapper Zeichen zu einem blitzschnell wiedererkennbaren Muster. In einem Leitartikel der Ullsteinpresse lässt sich 1927 die Berlinerin Käthe Marcus über „Die typisierte Frau" aus: Bubikopf, schlanke Linie, kurzer Rock. Diese auffällig veränderte, neue Grundform der Bekleidung sei überall gleich. „Die Gleichform" betreffe nicht nur Form-, Stoff- und Farbenwahl, sondern sei eine Normsetzung für alles, was man trage und wie man es trage. Das Bedürfnis der Gesellschaft der Zwischenkriegszeit, zu ordnen und aus vergleichbaren Gruppen die Standards sowie das Typische herauszufiltern, bezeichnet der Literaturwissenschaftler Helmut Lethen 1994 als „klirrenden Schematismus": Eine Angstreaktion auf die Verstörungen der Moderne, die in den Konturen eines in „konstruktiver Sachlichkeit" geformten weiblichen Körpers sichtbar wird.

51 Modegraphik / Fashion plate
Atelier Bachwitz, ca. 1925

52 Modezeichnung von Hete Behrens / Fashion drawing by Hete Behrens
Köln / Cologne, ca. 1930/31

The need felt by society in the years between the world wars to order everything and distil standards of what was typical from comparable groups was described in 1994 by Helmut Lethen, a historian of literature, as 'jangling schematicism': reacting with angst to Modernist unease, which becomes apparent in the contours of a female body shaped with 'constructive objectivity'.

53 Pullunder mit
Bundfaltenhose /
Jumper and slacks
Deutschland /
Germany, 1930/40

54 **Chiffonkleid /
Chiffon dress**
Lichtenberg/Ober-
franken / Lichtenberg/
Upper Franconia,
ca. 1933/37

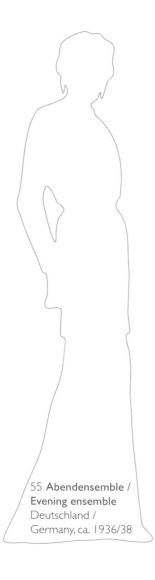

55 **Abendensemble /**
Evening ensemble
Deutschland /
Germany, ca. 1936/38

56 „Kleines
Schwarzes" /
'Little black
dress'
Deutschland /
Germany,
ca. 1945

57 **Abendkleid /**
Evening dress
Salon Stuckenberger
München / Munich,
ca. 1945/46

58 „Kleines
Schwarzes" /
'Little black
dress'
Wien oder
Königsberg /
Vienna or
Königsberg,
ca. 1945/47

59 **Sommer-Ensemble mit Hut /**
Summer ensemble with hat
Deutschland / Germany, ca. 1952

60 **Glockenrock mit Bluse /**
Flared skirt with blouse
Modehaus Horn
Berlin/Hamburg, ca. 1953/54

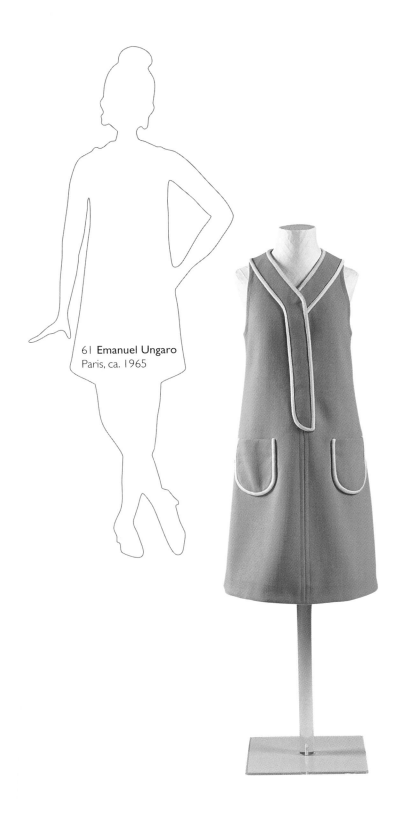

61 Emanuel Ungaro
Paris, ca. 1965

62 **Paco Rabanne**
Paris, ca. 1966/67

63 **Cocktailkleid /
Cocktail dress**
Ponater Modelle
München / Munich,
ca. 1967/69

64 Partykleid mit Op-Art-Muster /
Party dress with Op Art pattern
Boltze-Modell
Deutschland / Germany, ca. 1965/70

65 **Hosenanzug /
Trouser suit**
Deutschland / Germany,
ca. 1970

66 **Emilio Pucci**
Florenz / Florence,
ca. 1974/75

67 Yves Saint Laurent
Paris, 1984

68 **Ensemble aus Bluse, Rock und Schärpe /
Blouse, skirt and scarf**
Deutschland / Germany,
ca. 1980/81

69 Jean Paul Gaultier
Paris, 1984/85

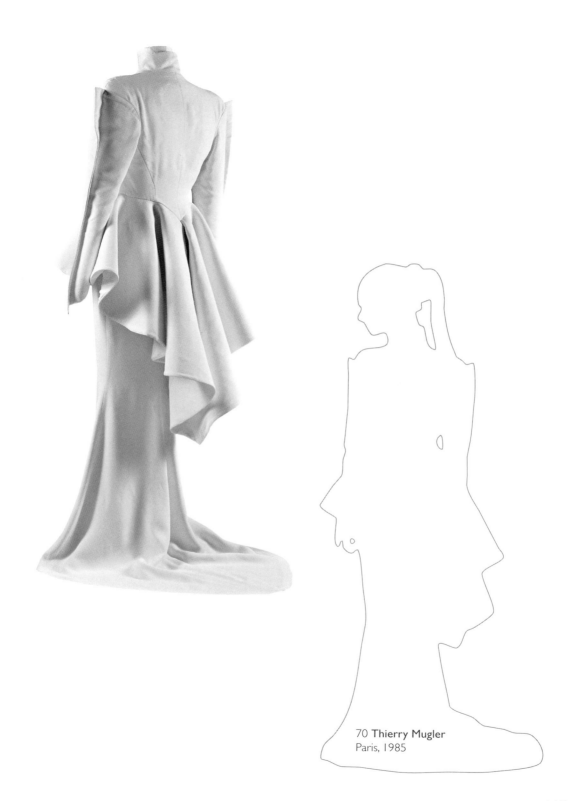

70 **Thierry Mugler**
Paris, 1985

71 **Azzedine Alaïa**
Paris, ca. 1985/87

116

72 **Moschino**
Mailand / Milan, ca. 1986/87

117

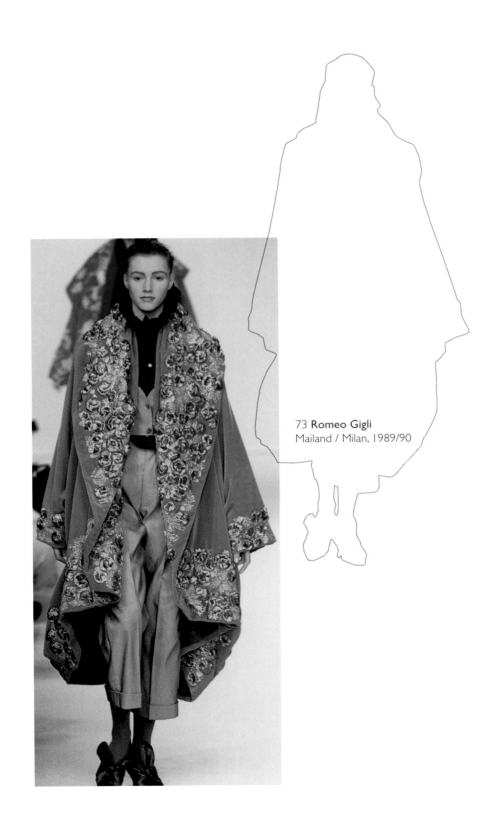

73 **Romeo Gigli**
Mailand / Milan, 1989/90

74 Vivienne
Westwood
London, ca. 1993

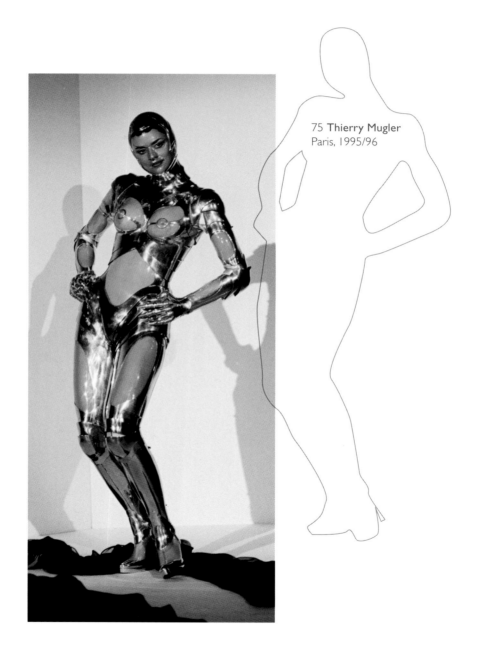

75 **Thierry Mugler**
Paris, 1995/96

76 Christian Dior
Paris, 1997/98

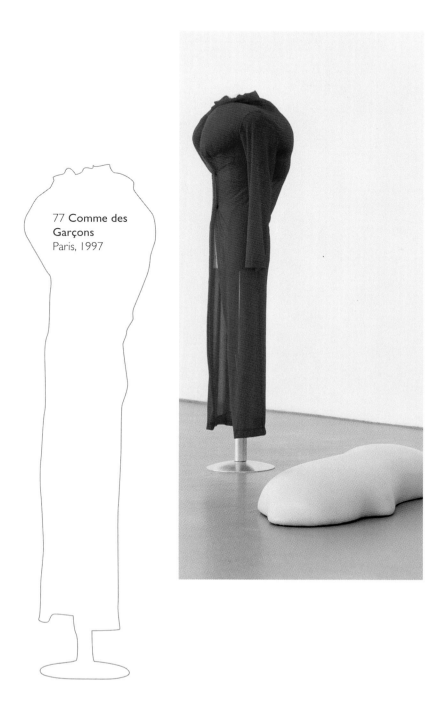

77 **Comme des Garçons**
Paris, 1997

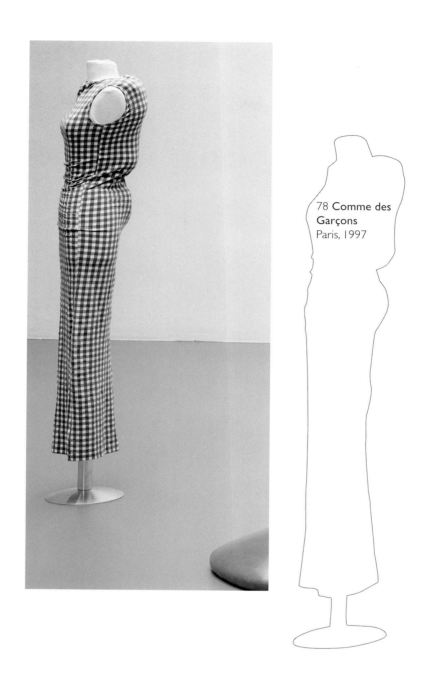

78 **Comme des Garçons**
Paris, 1997

Documenta Weiblichkeit

Die Bekleidung von Documenta-Besucherinnen
(1997 und 2002)

Ingrid Heimann

Wer bei Ludwig Gabriel Schrieber Bildhauerei studiert hat, und sei es auch nur wenige Semester, weiß sofort, was Modellierung des Weiblichen bedeutet. Wie man modelliert, wie es sich anfühlt und was zu sehen sein muss, vermittelte er wortlos mit seinem Daumen. Dieser breite Daumen strich fordernd über die bemühten Rundungen der studentischen Übungsarbeiten und fühlte nichts Plastisches. „Alles flach", murmelte er dann tief enttäuscht. Eine in jedem Punkt lebendig gespannte Rundung kam trotz verzweifelter Bemühungen der studentischen Modellierer selten zustande. Fast immer ertastete der verehrte Lehrer nur Flächen. Nach langen, quälenden Versuchen des Daumens, die im Luftraum gezogene Spannungslinie losgelöst von den Übungsarbeiten als ideales Vorbild wirksam werden zu lassen, konnte es vorkommen, dass er gebeugt und mutlos ins Nebenzimmer schlurfte und eine weibliche Figur auf einem Modellierbock hereinschob, damit alle Herumstehenden jetzt und für immer wissen sollten, was eine plastische Rundung sei.

Der hellsichtige Daumen strich nach einigem Zögern erklärend über die Figur. Die Schultern wurden durch ovale Schwünge beschrieben, die Brüste in allen Richtungen behaglich seufzend umrundet, der bergig glatte Bauch von den Tälern aus angegangen, der Venushügel, als plastisch gespanntes Dreieck vom Daumen besonders beachtet, die ausladenden, festen Hüftlinien unendlich oft nachgezogen. Alle Anwesenden sahen zuerst ungläubig und dann mit wachsend verschämter Freude die in jedem Punkt gespannt modellierten, lebendigen Formen des Weiblichen.

Im Sommersemester 1957 war das auch an der Staatlichen Hochschule für Bildende Künste in Berlin ein ungewöhnliches Ereignis. Mein weiter, faltiger Malerkittel, an dem ich anschließend forschend heruntersah, bildete eigene plastische Formen und verdeckte das eben eindrücklich erfahrene Weiblichkeitsbild vollkommen. Für einen kurzen Augenblick fühlte ich erschreckt und ablehnend die körperlich verändernde Gestalt des Kittels, um gleich darauf die geschlechtliche Neutralität zu preisen, die seine Formen erlaubten. Schon die Malweiber

Documenta Femaleness

Clothing worn by Women Documenta Visitors (1997 and 2002)

Ingrid Heimann

Anyone who has studied sculpture with Ludwig Gabriel Schrieber, even for only a few terms, knows immediately what modelling of femaleness is. Without uttering a word he would indicate with his thumb how modelling was to be done, what it felt like and how it had to look. That broad thumb stroked challengingly over the curves so conscientiously and laboriously created by students honing their skills and would encounter no plasticity at all. 'All flat', he would then mutter, thoroughly disappointed. A bouncy, taut curve emerged rarely, if ever, for all the desperate struggles of students aspiring to be modellers. Surfaces were all that their distinguished teacher almost invariably touched. After protracted, tortuous attempts with his thumb to draw a taut line in the air which, free of all practice attempts, might effectively become an ideal model, he would on occasion, bent and discouraged, shuffle without a word into the next room, only to return pushing a female figure on a modeller's block so that everyone standing about might learn for all time what a curve with plasticity was.

That clairvoyant thumb hesitated before stroking elucidatingly over the figure. The shoulders were described by oval sweeps, the curves of the breasts would be traced with a sigh of relief, the mountainous, smooth tummy approached from the valleys, with particular attention paid to the pubic mound as a taut, plastic triangle by that thumb and the broad yet firm hipline endlessly traced and retraced. All those present stared at first in disbelief but then gazed with growing, albeit, embarrassed, delight at the living form of femaleness thus stringently modelled at every point.

In summer term 1957 that was an unusual event, even for the Berlin Staatliche Hochschule für Bildende Künste. My generously cut, rumpled painting smock, which I then looked down at curiously, formed plastic shapes of its own, completely concealing the image of femaleness which had just been experienced with such immediacy. For a brief moment I felt alarmed, rejecting the form of the smock which changed the shape of my body but no sooner had I done so than I began to appreciate the gender neutrality afforded by its forms. Those painting females in 1900 had hidden their bodies beneath tent-like smocks in order to be

79 Stehende mit erhobenem Arm /
Woman standing, her arm raised
Ludwig Gabriel Schrieber, Berlin, 1955

um 1900 hatten ihren Körper unter zeltartigen Kitteln verborgen, um als selbständig handelnde, männerähnliche Personen wahr- und ernstgenommen zu werden.

Die bildreiche Doppellektion verdeutlicht: Der Körper bildet die plastische Realität.

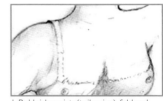

1 Bekleidung ist: (teilweise) fehlend
Clothing is: (partly) missing

Die Primärmodellierung des Körpers ist die Ausgangsplastizität für eine artifizielle Sekundärmodellierung. Die Kleider breiten sich in unterschiedlicher Gestalt, wechselndem Material und Volumen über die primären Körperformen aus. Die Sekundärmodellierung prägt und stellt sowohl eine gesellschaftliche als auch individuelle Nachricht über den Träger her. Die methodische Untersuchung dieser Körperveränderungen kann u.a. Rollenbilder, die das Verhältnis von Geschlecht und Zeit betreffen, verdeutlichen.

Fest umrissene Rahmenbedingungen (z.B. Übereinstimmung von Ort, Zeit, Klima, Geschlechter- und Altersverteilung) fördern klare Ergebnisse und sichern bei Vergleichen zutreffende und verwertbare Erkenntnisse. Die während der Documenta 1997 und 2002 aufgenommenen Fotoserien liefern eine hinreichende Menge von Beispielen (730) für die angestrebte vergleichende Analyse.

3 Bekleidung ist: (mittelbar) körpermeinend
Clothing is: (indirectly) referring to the body

Das Ziel ist, die typischen Modellierungen des gegenwärtigen Weiblichen als reale Formulierungen des weiblichen Selbstverständnisses durch eine Mengen- und Formanalyse des Verhältnisses von Körper und Bekleidung herauszuarbeiten. Es stellt sich folgende Frage: Wie und wie weit verändert die Sekundär- die Primärmodellierung? Der Vergleich wird an einem Beispiel erläutert, die Ergebnisse werden im Einzelnen und optisch nachvollziehbar dargestellt. Der ‚Modellierdaumen' dient hierbei als sinnlicher Wegweiser in Richtung weiblicher Körperorte.

Was ist mit den nackten, oval gerundeten Schultern zwischen 1997 und 2002 geschehen? Um die Veränderungen durch die Bekleidung

5 Bekleidung ist: (weitgehend) entkörperlichend
Clothing is: (largely) negating the body

taken seriously, in fact perceived at all, as mannish persons acting independently.

As that richly illustrated double lesson shows: it is the body that shapes
plastic reality.

2 Bekleidung ist: (überwiegend)
körperidentisch
Clothing is: (mostly) identical with the
body

The primary modelling of the body represents the initial plasticity for
an artificial secondary modelling. Clothes spread out in diverse forms,
different types of material and varying volumes over the primary body
forms. This secondary modelling shapes, thus formulating both a societal
and a personal message on the wearer. A methodical study of such body
changes can clarify, among other things, role images concerned with the
relationship between gender and time.

Firmly establishing parameters (e.g., correlations between place, time,
climate, gender and age distribution) promotes unequivocal results
and provides in comparison apposite and useful knowledge. The photo
sequences taken during Documenta 1997 and 2002 furnish a sufficient
number of examples (730) for the comparative analysis to be attempted.

4 Bekleidung ist: (nachvollziehbar)
körperverändernd
Clothing is: (comprehensibly) changing
the body

The objective is to ascertain the typical modellings of current femaleness
as real formulations of the female self-image by means of quantitative
and form analysis of the relationship between body and clothing. The
following question arises: how and to what extent does secondary
modelling modify primary modelling? The comparison will be explained
by an example. The results will be represented in a way that is both
individually and visually intelligible. The 'modelling thumb' will serve here
as a sensory guideline pointing to female body locations.

What happened to the naked, ovally rounded shoulder between 1997
and 2002? In order to elucidate more clearly the changes brought about
by clothing, clothing will be subdivided by type into five stages, to which
the clothing worn by women visitors to the exhibitions will be assigned.

besser veranschaulichen zu können, wird die Bekleidungsart in fünf Stufen eingeteilt, denen die realen Bekleidungen der Ausstellungs-Besucherinnen zugeordnet werden.

Die Schulterplastizität hat sich von 1997 bis 2002 deutlich verändert. Über die Hälfte der Schulterbekleidungen entspricht 1997 den Stufen 4 und 5, 2002 hingegen den Stufen 1 bis 3. Die dicken Polster, die man 1997 selbst durch dünne T-Shirts auf den Schultern ruhen sieht, über-mitteln, besonders da sie funktionell nicht zwingend erforderlich sind, unübersehbar die Nachricht, dass Frauen das Leben schultern können. Die ,Lebenshilfe' durch diese polsternde Aufmodellierung ist 2002 fast verschwunden. Das reale, kaum veränderte Schultergelenk (1 bis 3) signalisiert 2002, dass Frauen, so wie sie sind, das Leben schultern wollen.

Der abgebildete Torso ist eine Konzentration auf die körperliche Mitte. Von Kopf, Armen und Beinen unbeeinflusst, wird die sinnliche Existenz von Schultern, Brüsten, Bauch und Hüften zu einer unüber-sehbaren Realität. Die Bekleidungszonen der Besucherinnen werden den bereits grundsätzlich vorgestellten fünf Stufen zugeordnet. Die jeweiligen materialisierten Höchstbelegungen werden dem Torso halb übergezogen und veranschaulichen seine Veränderung. Die geraden, kantigen Schultern, die gemeinten, aber nicht betonten Brüste und Hüften ergeben 1997 ein zwiespältiges, teilweise verwischtes Körper-bild. Der hinter einem harten Brett verschwundene Bauch lässt keine Vorstellung von weiblicher Plastizität aufkommen.

Dies bedeutet, dass nicht nur die reine Veränderung des Volumens eine Rolle spielt, sondern u.a. auch bewusst Assoziationshinweise auf männ-liche Attribute (z.B. Waschbrettbauch und breite Schultern) herange-zogen werden, um der Sekundärmodellierung Nachrichtengenauigkeit zu verleihen. Das Frauenbild zur Zeit der Documenta von 1997 stellt sich somit im Sinne der 3. Emanzipationsstufe als ,beherrscht weiblich' und ,angestrebt stark' dar. Dagegen entfaltet sich 2002 eine andere Weiblichkeitsmodellierung, die sich schon 1997 in ,bekleidungsnahen'

1997
Schulter / Shoulder

1

10%

2

10%

3

23%

4

31%

5

26%

2002
Schulter / Shoulder

I

24%

2

23%

3

38%

4

13%

5

2%

Shoulder plasticity changed noticeably between 1997 and 2002. More than half of shoulder clothing in 1997 corresponds to stages 4 and 5, in 2002, on the other hand, to stages 1 to 3. Visible even through thin T-shirts, the thick padding resting on shoulders in 1997 transmitted the message, especially since there was no compelling functional reason for it, that women could shoulder the burdens of life. The 'aid to living' provided by this upholstering extra modelling had virtually disappeared by 2002. The real, almost unmodified shoulder joint (1 to 3) signalizes in 2002 that women want to shoulder the burdens of life but do so just as they are.

The torso shown concentrates on the middle of the body. Uninfluenced by head, arms and legs, the sensual existence of shoulders, breasts, tummy and hips becomes reality that cannot be overlooked. Women visitors' clothing zones are assigned to the five stages which have already been presented in essentials. The highest incidences that materialize in each instance are drawn half over the torso to show how it has changed. The straight, angular shoulderline, the breasts and hips hinted at but not emphasised breasts and hips imply in 1997 an ambivalent, partly blurred body image. A tummy which has disappeared behind a hard board does not permit any idea of female plasticity to emerge.

This means that not only does pure change in volume play a role but also, among other things, associative references to masculine attributes (e.g., a washboard stomach and broad shoulders) will be deliberately added to lend imaging precision to secondary modelling. The female image of the 1997 Documenta is consequently represented in terms of the 3rd stage of emancipation as 'controlled femininity' and 'aspiring to strength'. In 2002, on the other hand, a different female modelling develops, heralded as early as 1997 by groups 'close to the garment industry' (including young women studying design). Secondary and primary modelling rapidly begin to converge. Shoulders and the tummy are intended but not emphasised. Breasts and hips attain a high level of body identity. This is a statement both on form and content. Women who visit

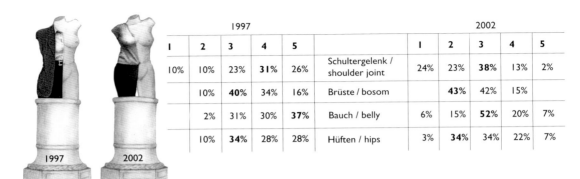

	1997						2002				
	1	2	3	4	5		1	2	3	4	5
	10%	10%	23%	**31%**	26%	Schultergelenk / shoulder joint	24%	23%	**38%**	13%	2%
		10%	**40%**	34%	16%	Brüste / bosom		**43%**	42%	15%	
		2%	31%	30%	**37%**	Bauch / belly	6%	15%	**52%**	20%	7%
		10%	**34%**	28%	28%	Hüften / hips	3%	**34%**	34%	22%	7%

1997 2002

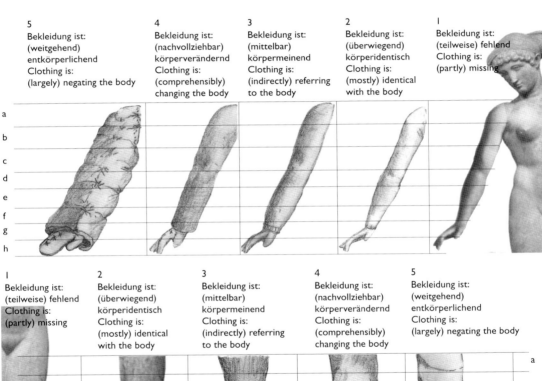

5
Bekleidung ist:
(weitgehend)
entkörperlichend
Clothing is:
(largely) negating the body

4
Bekleidung ist:
(nachvollziehbar)
körperverändernd
Clothing is:
(comprehensibly)
changing the body

3
Bekleidung ist:
(mittelbar)
körpermeinend
Clothing is:
(indirectly) referring
to the body

2
Bekleidung ist:
(überwiegend)
körperidentisch
Clothing is:
(mostly) identical
with the body

1
Bekleidung ist:
(teilweise) fehlend
Clothing is:
(partly) missing

a b c d e f g h

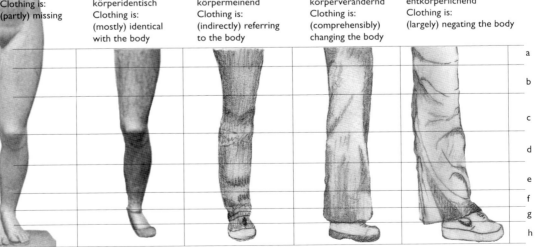

1
Bekleidung ist:
(teilweise) fehlend
Clothing is:
(partly) missing

2
Bekleidung ist:
(überwiegend)
körperidentisch
Clothing is:
(mostly) identical
with the body

3
Bekleidung ist:
(mittelbar)
körpermeinend
Clothing is:
(indirectly) referring
to the body

4
Bekleidung ist:
(nachvollziehbar)
körperverändernd
Clothing is:
(comprehensibly)
changing the body

5
Bekleidung ist:
(weitgehend)
entkörperlichend
Clothing is:
(largely) negating the body

a b c d e f g h

1997

	5	4	3	2	1
a	22%	**41%**	18%	5%	14%
b	22%	**40%**	19%	5%	14%
c	22%	**38%**	19%	1%	20%
d	22%	38%	4%	0%	**48%**
e	22%	38%	4%	0%	**51%**
f	17%	21%	4%	0%	**58%**
g	7%	5%	0%	0%	**88%**
h	0%	0%	0%	0%	**100%**

2002

	1	2	3	4	5
a	23%	29%	**31%**	17%	0%
b	27%	26%	**30%**	17%	0%
c	**50%**	8%	25%	17%	0%
d	**70%**	3%	14%	13%	0%
e	**78%**	1%	10%	11%	0%
f	**86%**	1%	3%	10%	0%
g	**93%**	0%	2%	5%	0%
h	**100%**	0%	0%	0%	0%

1997

	5	4	3	2	1
a	24%	34%	**35%**	7%	0%
b	18%	28%	**35%**	14%	5%
c	18%	19%	**35%**	19%	9%
d	13%	17%	**33%**	25%	12%
e	7%	17%	**31%**	29%	16%
f	2%	11%	27%	**34%**	26%
g	1%	9%	22%	**38%**	30%
h	0%	4%	40%	**56%**	0%

2002

	1	2	3	4	5
a	0%	27%	**33%**	25%	15%
b	3%	24%	**33%**	27%	13%
c	6%	21%	**33%**	28%	12%
d	16%	10%	**35%**	27%	12%
e	21%	8%	**30%**	29%	12%
f	**41%**	6%	16%	30%	7%
g	**39%**	8%	24%	22%	75
h	0%	39%	**50%**	9%	2%

80–95 Archiv Heimann /
Heimann archives

Gruppen (u.a. Designstudentinnen) ankündigte. Sekundärmodellierung und Primärmodellierung nähern sich rapide an. Schultern und Bauch sind gemeint, aber nicht herausgestellt. Brüste und Hüften erreichen eine hohe Körperidentität. Diese ist zugleich eine formale wie inhaltliche Aussage. Die Documenta-Besucherinnen gehen ‚selbstverständlich weiblich' und ‚mühelos stark' durch die Ausstellung.

Schulter, Brust, Bauch und Hüften werden als je eine Körperzone, die durch fünf Plastizitätsstufen verändert werden kann, erfasst. Die Längen von Arm und Hand sowie von Bein und Fuß bedingen, dass diese Körperteile in mehrere Körperzonen unterteilt werden. Die abgebildeten Schemata verbinden acht Körperzonen (a–h) mit den fünf bereits vorgestellten plastischen Modellierstufen zu einer Matrix. Jede reale Arm- oder Beinmodellierung stellt eine Auswahl aus den vierzig Elementen der Matrix dar, so dass ein bekleideter Arm z.B. aus den Elementen 4a oder 4c sowie 1d oder 1h bestehen kann.

Die beschriebenen Arm- und Beinraster bilden auch das Aufzeichnungsinstrument für die Analyseergebnisse. Die einzelnen realen Modellierstärken der Bein- und Armbekleidungen werden den jeweils vierzig Elementen zugeordnet. Ihre prozentuale Auswertung lässt die Bestimmung der Höchstbelegung zu. Die Ergebnisse werden ebenfalls in Tabellen anschaulich gemacht. Die Veränderung von 1997 zu 2002 verwundert nicht. Die Modellierung des Oberarms (a–c) von 1997 lässt den ganzen Arm bekleidet aussehen. 2002 dagegen herrscht Armnacktheit vor und wird zusätzlich von der Kürze des Ärmels unterstützt.

Bei der Beinbekleidung lassen die Höchstbelegungen eine leichte Stufenverschiebung von 1997 zu 2002 vor allem im Knöchelbereich erkennen. Die nackte Knöchelpartie macht das Gehen 2002 unmittelbarer und stellt die Knöchelaktivität heraus, der festere Schuh signalisiert sicheres Auftreten. In der Bekleidungsgeschichte spielte die auffallend sichtbar gemachte Knöchelpartie bei männlicher und weiblicher Beinbekleidung häufig eine Rolle (z.B. bei Mägde-Bekleidung), besonders wenn auf Fußaktivität hingewiesen werden sollte.

Documenta go through the exhibition 'taking femaleness for granted' and being 'effortlessly strong'.

The shoulder, breasts, tummy and hips are registered as separate body zones which can be modified by five stages of plasticity. The lengths of arm and hand as well as leg and foot require these parts of the body to be distributed over several body zones. The charts juxtaposed link eight body zones (a–h) with the five stages of plastic modelling introduced above to form a matrix. Each real arm or leg modelling represents a selection from the forty elements of the matrix so that a clothed arm can consist, say, in elements 4a or 4c as well as 1d or 1h.

The arm and leg grids described also furnish the instrument for recording the analysis results. The individual real modelling thicknesses of leg or arm clothing are assigned to forty elements respectively. Evaluating them in percentages makes it possible to determine the highest incidence figure. The results are also shown in tables. The change that took place between 1997 and 2002 is not surprising. The 1997 modelling of the upper arm (a–c) makes the entire arm look clothed. In 2002, on the other hand, arm nakedness predominates and is reinforced by sleeve shortness.

As far as legwear is concerned, the highest incidences reveal a slight shift in stage between 1997 and 2002, especially around the ankle. Naked ankles make going more immediate in 2002 and emphasize ankle activity; firmer shoes signalize confident appearance in public. In the history of clothing, obviously bared ankles in both men's and women's legwear often play a role (for instance in the clothing worn by female domestics), especially when pedal activity is to be underscored.

Erstaunlich ist 2002, erkennbar auch schon 1997, die Überlänge der Hosen und eine Verdickung im Knöchelbereich. Die Beinbekleidungen der Besucherinnen sind darüber hinaus aber zu formenreich, so dass sich nur allgemeine Tendenzen ableiten lassen, jedoch keine spezifischen Informationen über die Gestalt gezogen werden können.

So viel Formenumfang und Formenmut während eines begrenzten Zeitraumes hat die Menge der weiblichen Beine auch im historischen Vergleich, soweit dieser möglich ist, noch nie gezeigt. Weibliches Im-Leben-Stehen, Auftreten, Vorwärtskommen, Ankommen erfahren durch die Darstellungsfülle individuelle und allgemeine Nachrichtenrealität. Der ausgedehnte Formenumfang zeugt gleichzeitig von der Herausforderung, die aktuellen gesellschaftlichen und formalen Möglichkeiten zu beherrschen. Wenn Formenreichtum Informationsintensität erzeugt, dann vermittelt er hier Seh-, Bekleidungs- und Lebenslust.

Die vorangegangene, vorwiegend optische Analyse soll abschließend ebenfalls in einem Bild zusammengefasst werden: Eine junge Frau sitzt in einem sonst leeren Durchgangsraum der Ausstellung auf dem Boden. Sie kümmert sich nicht um die Besucherscharen, die unentwegt an ihr vorbeiziehen, und auch nicht um die begeisterte Fotografin. Aufmerksam sortiert sie bereits Geschriebenes und denkt dabei über weitere Formulierungen nach. Die Arbeit am Ausstellungsort hat sie sorgfältig geplant. Ein dickes, rundes Kissen, das sie in ihrem Rucksack mitgebracht hat, macht längeres Sitzen auf dem Boden möglich. Sie ist barhäuptig. Eine dünne Bluse, die so kurz ist, dass sie einen Streifen von Taille und Bauch sehen lässt, formuliert die körperliche Mitte als selbstbewusst weiblich. Der Arm ist frei, die Hand greift zu. Dem allgemeinen Formenreichtum der weiblichen Beinbekleidung kann sie eine bezeichnende Variante hinzufügen. Die aufgekrempelten und unterschiedlich hoch gerutschten Hosenbeine demonstrieren ungezwungene Variabilität.

What is astonishing in 2002 is trouser legs being worn extra long and the thickening of material in the ankle region. This was already showing up in 1997. Moreover, the legwear of women visiting the exhibition is so diverse in form that only general tendencies can be inferred yet no specific conclusions on form can be drawn.

Such a variety of forms and the courage to wear those forms during such a limited time span has, even in historical comparisons (in so far as this is possible) never before been shown by the sum of female legs. Female being-involved-in-life, appearing confidently in public, making progress, arriving: all achieve through the representational quantity both individual and general imaging reality transmitting a message. The large quantity of forms attests at the same time to the challenge of mastering current societal opportunities and formal possibilities. When a wealth of forms generates information intensity, it follows that it is here conveying pleasure in seeing and being seen, wearing clothes and simply joie de vivre.

The mainly visual analysis outlined above can in conclusion be summarised in another picture: a young woman is sitting on the floor of an otherwise empty passage room at the exhibition. She is paying no attention at all to the throngs of visitors continually passing her by and she ignores the woman enthusiastically photographing her. She is concentrating on sorting out what she has written and is thinking over other ways of expressing it. She has carefully planned her work at the exhibition venue. A thick round cushion which she has brought with her in her rucksack enables her to sit longer on the floor. She wears nothing on her head. A thin blouse, which is so abbreviated that it reveals strips of waist and tummy, formulates the centre of her body as self-confidently female. Her arm is free, her hand grasps. She can now add a signalizing variant to the overall diversity of female legwear. Her trouser legs, rolled up and pushed to different levels, demonstrate casual variability.

Die junge Frau steht exemplarisch für die Frau im Jahr 2002, wie sie auch durch die Untersuchungsergebnisse dieser Bekleidungsanalyse beschrieben wird. Gegenüber der Frau im Jahr 1997 erweist sie sich als selbstbewusster; die Mode ermöglicht ihr ein direkteres Körpergefühl, was ihrer Unabhängigkeit und Tatkraft entspricht.

Text, Fotos, Abbildungsgestaltung und Statistik Ingrid Heimann

(Archiv Heimann, Berlin)

This young woman exemplifies woman in 2002 as she has been described by the results of the clothing analysis outlined here. She is more self-confidant than the 1997 woman; fashion has empowered her with a more immediate feeling for her own body, which matches her independence and energy.

Text, photos, illustration design and statistics: Ingrid Heimann (Archiv Heimann, Berlin)

96 **Walter van Beirendonck**
Antwerpen / Antwerp, 1997

97 **Dries van Noten**
Antwerpen /
Antwerp,
1998

98 **Hussein Chalayan**
London, 1998

99 Christian Dior
Paris, ca. 1999

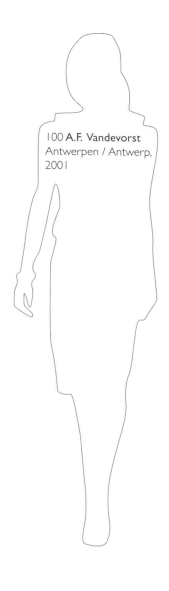

100 **A.F. Vandevorst**
Antwerpen / Antwerp,
2001

101 Elternhaus®
Maegde u. Knechte®
Hamburg, 2001

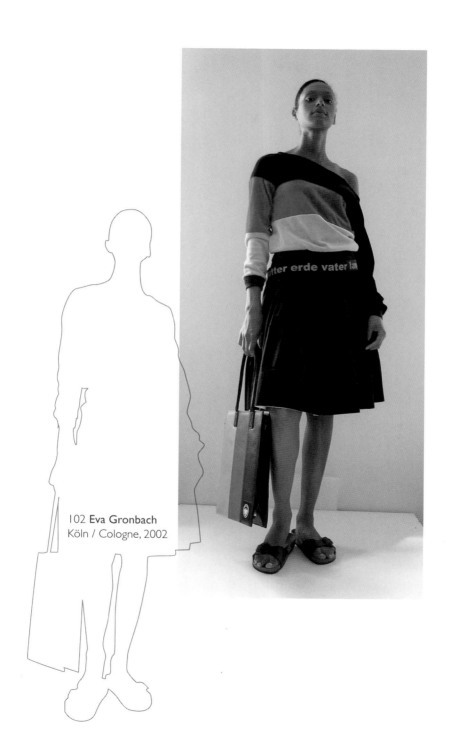

102 **Eva Gronbach**
Köln / Cologne, 2002

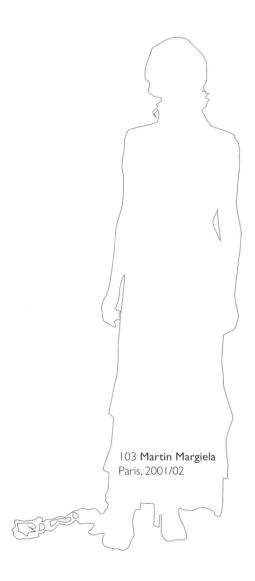

103 **Martin Margiela**
Paris, 2001/02

104 **Martin Margiela**
Paris, 2001/02

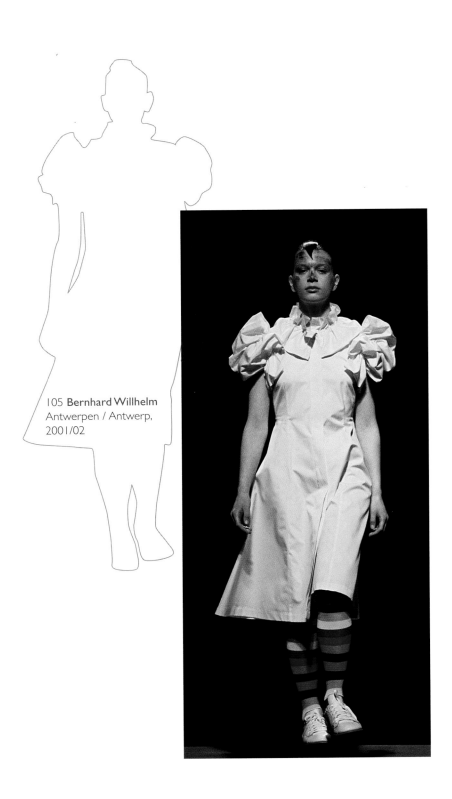

105 **Bernhard Willhelm**
Antwerpen / Antwerp,
2001/02

106 **Darja Richter**
Paris, 2002/03

107 **Strenesse**
Gabriele Strehle
Nördlingen, 2002/03

108 **Strenesse**
Gabriele Strehle
Nördlingen, 2002/03

Vom Saum zum Bündchen – Körperkonstruktionen und Geschlechterinszenierungen

Uta Brandes

Es ist klar: Körper und Mode hängen unauflöslich zusammen. Nicht so klar allerdings ist, ob die Mode am Körper oder der Körper an der Mode hängt. Der Körper war – neben dem sozialen – immer auch geschlechtlicher Körper. Mode, das ist hinlänglich bekannt, folgte gesellschaftlichen Funktionen und tribalen, ständischen oder klassenspezifischen Hierarchien, die wiederum grundsätzlich in jeder sozialen Gruppe auch nach Geschlecht differierten. Die erste Zäsur erfuhren die Körper seit dem späten 17. und frühen 18. Jahrhundert. Von nun an ist der Körper nicht mehr einfach, sondern man *hat* ihn.[1] Und heute ist vieles noch ganz anders: Wir stellen Geschlecht aktiv, jeden Tag (neu) her.[2] Was früher durch den geschlechtlich konnotierten Habit auf den ersten Blick kenntlich war, weicht heute einer immer größeren Variabilität der Kleidung und damit einhergehender Verunsicherung der Geschlechtsmarkierungen, weil wir unseren Geschlechtskörper durch Mode überhöhen, inszenieren, ‚veruneindeutigen', verstecken, parodieren, etc. können. Ein Paradoxon: Während historisch bereits der verhüllte Körper biologisch eindeutig gekennzeichnet war, muss er im 21. Jahrhundert – wie einst bei Adam und Eva, nachdem Eva vom Baum der Erkenntnis gegessen und Adam zu ebensolchem Handeln verführt hatte – zur primären geschlechtlichen Identifizierung wieder vollständig entblößt werden. Mode gibt jedenfalls keine verlässlichen Hinweise mehr auf das biologische Geschlecht.

Dieses Spiel mit dem Geschlechtskörper durch entsprechende Drapierungen scheint uns, auf andere bezogen, aber durchaus Probleme zu bereiten. Denn Alltagskommunikation braucht die Sicherheit zu wissen, wer der oder die andere ist, Geschlecht muss dingfest gemacht werden. Deshalb fragen Jung und Alt, wenn sie einen Säugling erblicken, unisono und als erstes: „Wie niedlich – was ist es denn – Junge oder Mädchen?". Sofern ein Gegenüber nicht sofort als entweder Mann oder Frau zu dechiffrieren ist (und da es als sehr unhöflich gilt, direkt nach der Geschlechtszugehörigkeit zu fragen), werden Zeichen zu deuten gesucht: Körperhaltung, Gestik, Stimme etc., die das Geschlecht identifizieren könnten.

109–114 Lilith & Burkhard im Museum für Angewandte Kunst Köln, Juli 2003 /
Lilith & Burkhard in the Museum of Applied Art Cologne, July 2003

From Hemline to Waistline –
Body Construct and Gender Staging

Uta Brandes

It's obvious: the body and fashion are indissolubly intertwined. What isn't so obvious is whether fashion depends on the body or the body on fashion. The body has always been – apart from being a social entity – a gender entity. Fashion, as is sufficiently well-known, has followed societal functions as well as tribal, professional or class-specific hierarchies, which in turn have differed fundamentally depending on social group as well as gender. Bodies experienced the first hiatus from the late 17th and early 18th century. From then on the body no longer simply *existed*; one *had* a body.[1] And nowadays many things are entirely different: we actively (re)create gender every day.[2] What used to be recognisable at first sight as gender-connoting dress has yielded today to an increasing variability of clothing and has, concomitantly, resulted in loss of assurance about gender markers. This is so because we can heighten our gender bodies by means of fashion, we stage, render them 'ambiguous', hide, parody them, etc. This is paradoxical. On the one hand, from the historical angle, the wrapped up body was already marked as biologically unambivalent. In the 21st century, on the other hand, the body will once again – as happened to Adam and Eve after Eve had partaken of the Tree of Knowledge and seduced Adam to do likewise – have to be entirely exposed to make primary sexual characteristics identifiable. Fashion is, in any case, no longer a reliable indicator of biological gender.

This game played with the gender body by draping it accordingly seems to us, in reference to others, however, to cause considerable difficulties. After all, for everyday communication one must be assured of knowing whether one's opposite number is a he or a she: gender must be established beyond all doubt. Consequently, the first thing young and old do on sighting an infant is to coo with one voice: 'How cute – what is it – a boy or a girl?' Should one be unable to decode the gender of one's opposite number (and, since it is regarded as uncourteous to ask about gender directly), signs are sought which might give a clue as to gender identification: body language, gestures, voice, etc.

Wohlgemerkt: Die Frage nach sexuellen Orientierungen und Präferenzen spielt hier noch gar keine Rolle. Und dennoch ist die Vorstellung, in der unverbindlichsten, scheinbar von keinerlei Erotik getrübten Small-Talk-Situation, mit einer biologisch nicht geschlechtsidentifizierten Person zu reden, schwer zu ertragen und würde die Kommunikation ohne Zweifel beeinflussen, verunsichern.

Seit die soziale Konstruktion von Männlichkeit und Weiblichkeit, wie sie immer auch explizit durch polare Körpergestaltung (Frisur, Kleidung, Accessoires) trennend hervorgehoben wurde, einer tiefgreifenden Körper- und Hüllendiversifikation unterworfen wird, existieren körperliche und modische 'Paralleluniversen'. Womit keineswegs behauptet werden soll, es handele sich hierbei um die Freiheit der Individuen, autonom über ihre Körperinszenierungen entscheiden zu können. Trotz der Vielgestaltigkeit herrschen Zwänge und globale Corporate Identities. Wie für Unternehmen gilt dies auch für den Menschen: Er darf heute viel mehr – bei avancierten Firmen heißt das „offene CI" –, aber er muss auch überwältigend viel sowohl Performation als auch moderne Anpassung betreiben. Große, sich modern wähnende Unternehmen etwa haben den „casual day" zur Pflicht erhoben. Freitags darf Mann nicht, sondern muss Mann ohne Krawatte und in Jeans zur Arbeit erscheinen, Frau gern bauchnabelfrei und in engem T-Shirt. Die sogenannten „kreativen" Branchen hingegen verlangen jederzeit schwarzes Outfit, unbedingt ohne Krawatte, Frau gern in enger Kleidung und spitzen high heels, manchmal auch Nike- und Adidas-gestählt.

Die Paralleluniversen der Mode beziehen sich auf die Gleichzeitigkeit verschiedener Modellierungen eines einzigen Körpers. Was früher als schlichte Alternative etwa zwischen Alltags- und Sonntagshabit erschien, ist heute einer er- oder überforderten Vielgesichtigkeit gewichen. Eine Person gehört nicht mehr nur einer einzigen modischen Zielgruppe, sondern so vielen gleichzeitig an, dass der Begriff obsolet wird.

Bear in mind, though: the question of sexual orientation and inclination do not yet play a role in this. Still the idea of conversing with a person of biologically as yet indeterminate gender, even in a small-talk situation seemingly free of erotic overtones, is difficult to put up with and this uncertainty would undoubtedly influence the tenor of communication and lead to uneasiness.

'Parallel universes' of physiology and fashion have existed as long as the social construct of masculine and feminine. They have been discriminately and even explicitly emphasised through bipolarity of body styling (hair-style, clothing, accessories) and subjected to a divergence of body and envelope that is far-reaching in its implications. This is not to say that what is concerned is the freedom of individuals to decide autonomously for themselves how to stage-manage their own bodies. For all the diversity of body styling available, constraints and global corporate identities are the order of the day. What is true of business also holds for people: nowadays we are permitted a lot more – in the business jargon of pro-gressive companies this is called 'open CI' – but we must also do an overwhelming amount of performing as well as modern adapting. Big companies, thinking they owe it to themselves to be modern, have desig-nated 'dress-down days' on which casual attire is de rigeur. On Fridays it isn't that a man may, he must appear at work without a tie and wearing jeans and she is encouraged to turn up flaunting her navel and sporting a skimpy T-shirt. The so-called 'creative' professions, on the other hand, adhere to a dress-code, require men to dress entirely in black at all times but definitely without a tie, with women preferred in tight-fitting clothing and teetering on pointy high heels, sometimes even underpinned with Nike or Adidas.

The parallel universes of fashion are related to a synchronicity of various modulations of a single body. What used to appear as a simple option between everyday and Sunday dress has yielded nowadays to required or demanded epiphenomenal sophistication. A person no longer belongs to a single fashion target market but instead to so many simultaneously that the term has become obsolete.

Wir alle tragen mannigfache Gesinnungen und Verortungen durch die Welt: den Arbeits-, Shopping-, Party-, Single-, Familien-, Fitness-, Wellness-, Abenteuer-Körper etc., der dementsprechend eingekleidet ist. „So viel Körper war nie", mögen wir da ebenso berechtigt wie besorgt mit Silvia Bovenschen ausrufen.[3] Die weiblichen idealisierten Körperbilder reichen von anorektischen und bulimischen über knabenhaft-androgyne bis zu Barbie-ähnlichen. Wobei diese Imaginationen sowohl psychische Probleme (Essstörungen) anzeigen als auch fast unmögliche körperliche Stählungen erfordern (großer Busen, Apfelpo, aber sehr schmale Taille sind ein Widerspruch in sich) oder permanenter Esskontrolle und vielen Trainings bedürfen. Zunehmend jedoch – und auch das ist ein Indikator für veränderte Geschlechterkonstruktionen – gibt es auch bei Männern fitness- oder magersüchtige Tendenzen, oder sie verfallen dem Trend zur Schönheitschirurgie.

Den heutigen modischen Inszenierungen ist ein Phänomen gemeinsam: Entschieden sich im gesamten 20. Jahrhundert die weiblichen Modetrends in erster Linie am Rocksaum (Maxi, Midi, Mini, „Po-Manschette"), ist es inzwischen das Bündchen, an dem alles hängt. Nicht der Saum schiebt sich nach oben, sondern das Bündchen oder die Taille rutschen nach unten. Galt zuvor die Länge des sichtbaren Beines als aufregend, starren wir nun fasziniert auf Taille, Bauch – und mittlerweile auf den Po- und Schamansatz, denn das Hosen- oder Rockbündchen entblößt diese bereits oder zieht den Blick auf einen tiefsitzenden, gleichwohl bewusst-kess herauslugenden Höschen- oder String-Ansatz. Die erotischen Körperteile, von denen das Auge einen Blick zu erhaschen sucht, sind übrigens dieselben geblieben: je nach Standpunkt geht es um die Scham oder um die Pobacken. Während jedoch im 20. Jahrhundert der Blick von unten nach oben wanderte, tut er dies nun von oben nach unten. Diese Saum- und Bündchendifferenz hat Auswirkungen auf die Geschlechter.

We all carry about with us a burden of multifarious ideologies and orientations everywhere we go: work, shopping, party, single, family, fitness, wellness, adventure bodies, etc., each clothed accordingly. 'There has never been so much body', we may feel justified in proclaim with Silvia Bovenschen and just concerned enough to do so.[3] Idealised female body images range from the anorectic and bulimic and the boyishly-androgynous to Barbie-Doll curvaceousness. These fantasies reveal both psychological problems (eating disorders) and virtually impossible bodily interventions (big tits and apple cheeks combined with a wasp waist represent a contradiction in terms) or require unrelenting control over diet coupled with relentless training sessions. Increasingly, however – and this, too, is an indicator of changes in gender constructs – men, too, are showing signs of fitness obsession or anorectic tendencies and they have even fallen prey to the plastic surgery mystique.

All fashion stagings nowadays have one phenomenon in common. Throughout the 20th century, feminine fashion trends primarily had to decide on hem lengths (Maxi, Midi, Mini, 'bum-huggers'). Now, by contrast, everything depends on the waistband. Hemlines are no longer creeping up; waistlines are slipping down. The length of leg visible used to titillate but today we stare in fascination at waists and bellies – and have arrived by now at cheek creases and pubic hair since trouser waistbands and skirt waistlines are already exposing them to view or our gaze is allured to plunge below the deliberately provocative line drawn way down where hotpants or thong begins. The erogenous zones which the eye is lusting for have, incidentally, remained the same: depending on one's vantage-point, the pudenda or the buttocks. Whereas the gaze wandered from bottom to top in the 20th century, it is now roaming in the opposite direction. The hem/waistline differential has an impact on gender.

War die Saumfrage ausschließlich eine des weiblichen Geschlechts (denn Röcke für Männer haben sich in der Moderne trotz aller modischen Versuche nie durchsetzen lassen, Schotten ausgenommen), ist die Bündchenhöhe für beide Geschlechter von Interesse, gleichwohl qualitativ und quantitativ in unterschiedlicher Weise. Die tiefsitzenden und häufig den Slipansatz enthüllenden männlichen Hosen werden fast ausschließlich von Jugendlichen und jungen Männern getragen, die sich der Hip-Hop-Bewegung zugehörig fühlen. Diese Hosen müssen außerdem so tun, als ob sie wie eine normale Hose aus Versehen weit heruntergerutscht seien, weshalb die Gesäßebene nun unnütz weit ausladend in der Kniekehle wackelt. Tiefsitzende Röcke und Hosen für Frauen umfassen eine viel größere Altersgruppe, sind nicht auf eine ‚Community' festgelegt und dürfen auf gar keinen Fall rutschen; denn sie sind hauteng und heben das Po-Areal deutlich hervor.

Diese Mode und die heutigen Körpervorstellungen insgesamt bedingen erst einmal für beide Geschlechter, eine ex- und intensive Beschäftigung mit ihren physischen Körpern: sie zu trimmen, zu quälen, zu zerren und zu stauchen, um unter anderem gestählte und flache bis konkav gewölbte Bäuche ihr eigen zu nennen. Über dem Hosen- oder Rockbündchen schwabbelnde Bäuche ohne Taille entsprechen eigentlich nicht dem strengen Körperregime und müssen ausgegrenzt werden. Die Körperideale und ihre zweiten Häute sind so widersprüchlich und verwirrend wie nie. Geschlecht wird inszeniert, perforiert, neutralisiert, androgynisiert, systematisiert und aufgelöst. Was wir heute vorfinden, sind körperliche Paralleluniversen, die zutiefst widersprüchlich sind: Da stehen Körperangst und Körperkult, Körperverdrängung und Körperaufwertung nebeneinander, aber auch Imaginationen von Körperauflösung. Und so ist vorläufig abschließend zu konstatieren: „Nicht mehr Kleider, sondern Körper machen Leute".[4]

Die eingangs formulierte Frage, ob die Mode am Körper oder aber dieser an jener hängt, erscheint unter solcher Perspektive nicht mehr als zu entscheidende Alternative, sondern als vertracktes Ineinander von beidem: Die Mode hängt als vielfältiges Aperçu an einem Körper,

The hemline issue was a purely feminine one (after all, skirts for men, despite all attempts by fashionistas to introduce them, have never taken, except in Scotland) but waistlines are interesting to both sexes, albeit in qualitatively and quantitatively different ways. Trousers cut so low they reveal the tops of underpants are worn almost exclusively by adolescents and young men who feel drawn to hiphop. Pants like these also have to pretend they have slipped down too far as if by accident, which could happen to any respectable pair of trousers, and this makes the baggy seat bulge uselessly about the knees. Low-cut skirts and trousers for women, on the other hand, appeal to a much larger target market. They are confined neither so narrowly to a particular age group nor to a 'community' and they are certainly not supposed to slip down since, just because they are skin-tight, they noticeably emphasize the bottom anyway.

This fashion and today's overall body image have first and foremost made both sexes extensively and intensively preoccupied with their physique: trimming it, torturing it, pulling or pummelling it into proper shape in order to reveal a washboard tummy or even a concavity where the tummy should be. Flabby bellies wobbling over waistlines, be they pants or skirt waistlines, do not tally with today's strict physical regimen and have to be done away with. The ideals governing the body and its second skin are more contradictory and confusing than ever before. Gender is being stage-managed, pierced, neutralised, androgynised, systematised and dissolved. What we encounter today are parallel universes which are profoundly contradictory. Body angst and body cult, compulsive body repression and body enhancement are all juxtaposed with ideas of bodily dissolution. And so all there is left to say for the time being is: 'Clothes no longer maketh man; bodies maketh man'.[4]

The question asked at the beginning of whether fashion depends on the body or vice versa no longer seems a crucial option when viewed from this angle. Instead it looks like an intractable interrelationship. Fashion depends as an aperçu on a body which is continually re-inventing itself with all the tricks of the trade as gender body. And the body depends on

der sich selbst als Geschlechtskörper finten- und variantenreich ständig neu erfindet. Und der Körper hängt an der Mode, weil er nur dadurch den stilisierten und getrimmten Geschlechtskörper zum Vorschein bringen kann. Nicht mehr Modellierungen von entweder Männlichkeit oder Weiblichkeit durch Mode finden statt, sondern es treten an ihre Stelle sowohl Geschlechtsmodellierungen, -konstruktionen als auch Geschlechterverwischungen. Die englische Sprache verbreitet noch die Gewissheit eines alternativen Entweder-Oder: entweder körperhafte Anwesenheit (somebody) oder Abwesenheit (nobody). Zukünftig werden wir womöglich simultane Geschlechts- und Körperwörter (er-)finden müssen.

[1] Diese Formulierung erinnert an die frühe Habeaskorpusakte von 1679, wonach kein englischer Untertan ohne gerichtliches Siegel verhaftet oder in Haft gehalten werden darf. – Ein recht früher Schutz des unversehrten Körpers (lat. „habeas corpus" = du habest den Körper), sozusagen die erste Anerkennung von Privatheit als vor staatlicher Willkür zu schützendes Gut. Sobald der Körper aber zum Gut, also zum Besitz wird, muss man auf ihn achten, ihn beherrschen (Gesundheitsbewusstsein und Triebkontrolle). Vgl. Norbert Elias: Über den Prozeß der Zivilisation. 2 Bde. Frankfurt/M. 1976.

[2] Vgl. Judith Butler: Das Unbehagen der Geschlechter (Frankfurt/M. 1991), die den anschaulichen Begriff des „doing gender" erstmals geprägt hat.

[3] Silvia Bovenschen: Soviel Körper war nie. In: Die Zeit, 14.11.1997, S. 63f.

[4] Gabriele Klein: Der Körper als Erfindung. In: Gero von Randow (Hrsg.): Wie viel Körper braucht der Mensch? Hamburg 2001, S. 61.

fashion because only through fashion is the stylised and trimmed gender body revealed. No longer do modulations of either masculine or feminine occur through fashion. They have been replaced by both gender modulations and constructs and gender blurring. The English language may still disseminate the certainty of an either–or option: either corporeal presence (somebody) or absence (nobody). In future we may have to (in)vent words that are both gender and body-related.

[1] This way of expressing it recalls the old Habeas Corpus Act of 1679, which ensured that no subject of the Crown might be arrested without a warrant issued by a court nor kept in prison without trial. – Quite an early example of safeguarding the body unharmed (Latin subjunctive sing. 'habeas corpus' = you must have the body), as it were, the first recognition of privacy as something beneficial to be protected from statist arbitrariness. As soon as the body becomes goods, that is, a possession, one has to care for it and master it (health consciousness and control of bodily urges). Cf. Norbert Elias: Über den Prozeß der Zivilisation. 2 vols. Frankfurt/M. 1976.
[2] Cf. Judith Butler: Das Unbehagen der Geschlechter. Frankfurt/M. 1991. She coined the graphic concept of 'doing gender'.
[3] Silvia Bovenschen: Soviel Körper war nie. In: Die Zeit, 14 Nov 1997, p. 63f.
[4] Gabriele Klein: Der Körper als Erfindung. In: Gero von Randow (ed.): Wie viel Körper braucht der Mensch? Hamburg 2001, p. 61.

115 **CHANEL**
Paris, 2003

116 **Christian Dior**
Paris, 2003

117–118 Jean Paul Gaultier
Paris, 2003

119 **Stephan Schneider**
Antwerpen / Antwerp,
2003

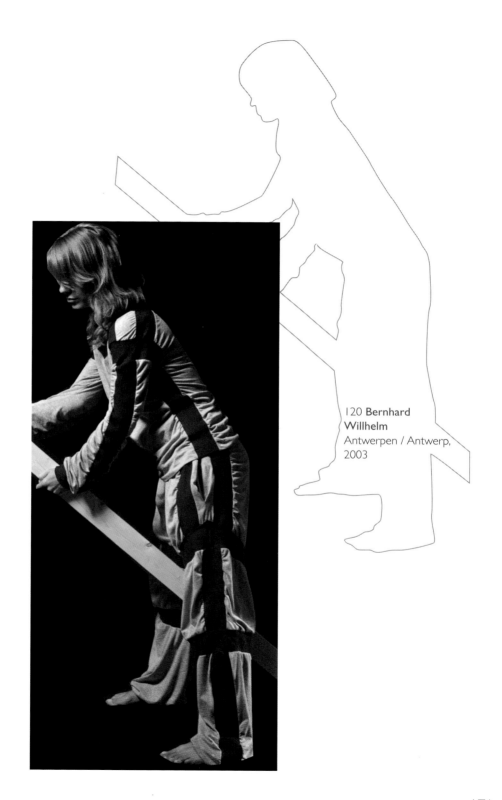

120 **Bernhard
Willhelm**
Antwerpen / Antwerp,
2003

121 **goyagoya**
Darmstadt, 2003

122 **Strenesse**
Gabriele Strehle
Nördlingen, 2003/04

123 **Hermès**
Paris, 2003/04

124 **Romeo Gigli**
Mailand / Milan, 2003/04

125 **Liz Weinmann**
Köln / Cologne, 2003/04

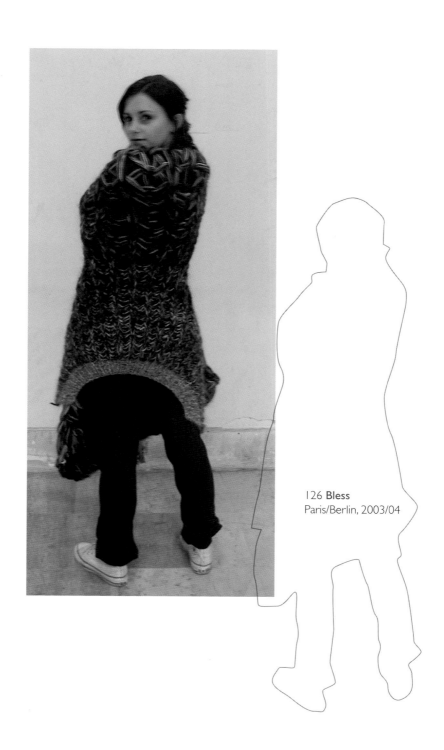

126 **Bless**
Paris/Berlin, 2003/04

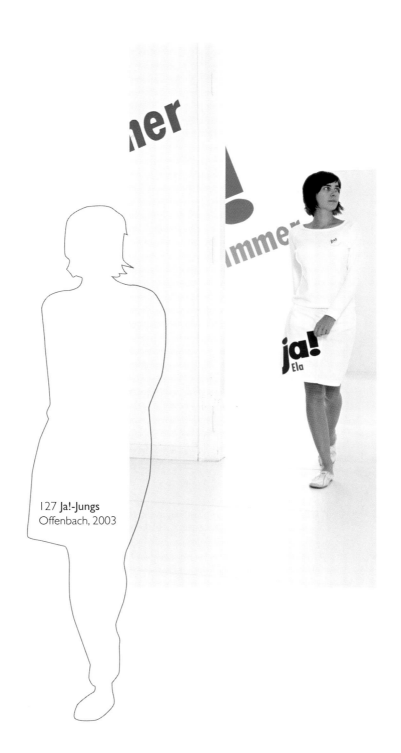

127 **Ja!-Jungs**
Offenbach, 2003

128 **Lutz**
Paris, 2003/04

Modeschöpfer ziehen an!

Interview mit der Designerin Eva Gronbach

Eva, was willst du in dieser Ausstellung zeigen?

Ich will Silhouetten zeigen, die mich geprägt haben.

Also nur eine „Eva-Auswahl"?

Ja und Nein. Man kann eben nur mit seinen eigenen Augen sehen. Trotzdem steht meine Auswahl für die Sicht meiner Generation – der „Generation Golf", die Wolfgang Florian Illies so wunderbar beschrieben hat. Jeder Mensch hat besondere Fähigkeiten. Meine liegt darin, zu erkennen, was der jeweilige Zeitgeist zu bedeuten hat. Man könnte sagen, dass ich die wesentlichen

129–131 Diana Gärtner in der Deutschen Botschaft in Paris / Diana Gärtner at the German embassy in Paris
Eva Gronbach, 2000

Trends der Zeit wie in einer Überschau darstelle. Aber man soll sich nicht täuschen: Die Sicht auf die Welt ist immer subjektiv. Objektivismus ist eine Lüge. Trotzdem bin ich Profi genug, um in meine „Vorzeit", die frühen 1980er Jahre zu blicken, die im Nachklang natürlich ebenfalls meine Umwelt beeinflusst haben.

Du bist als Designerin in vielen Ländern gewesen und hast bei vielen Firmen gearbeitet, prägt auch diese Erfahrung deine Auswahl?

Ganz sicher. Ich bin eine deutsche Europäerin. Ich bin in Deutschland aufgewachsen und in Europa zu Hause. Meine Arbeit im europäischen Ausland bei verschiedenen Designern hat mir einen Einblick in die internationale Modeszene verschafft. Nun will ich diese Sichtweise weitergeben. Eine Möglichkeit ist diese Ausstellung.

Du hast vorher gesagt „Objektivismus ist eine Lüge". Ich habe den Eindruck, dass die Auswahl deiner Silhouetten sich sehr stark an den Persönlichkeiten der Designer und ihrer gestalterischen Umsetzung des Zeitgeistes orientiert.

Fashion Designers Dress!

An Interview with the Designer Eva Gronbach

Eva, what are you trying to demonstrate in this exhibition?

I want to show silhouettes that have shaped me.

So, then, just 'Eva's Choice'?

Yes and no. You can only see with your own eyes. Still my choice stands for the way my generation sees things – the 'Golf Generation', which Wolfgang Florian Illies has described so marvellously. Every person has their own particular abilities. Mine is the ability to recognize what the Zeitgeist means at any given time. You might say that I represent the major trends of the times like a survey. But don't fool yourself. The way the world sees is always subjective. Objectivism is a lie. Nevertheless, I'm enough of a professional to be able to look back to my 'prehistory', the early 1980s, which of course has had repercussions for my environment.

As a designer you've been in many countries and worked for many companies; has this experience also affected your choice?

Certainly. I'm a German and a European. I grew up in Germany and I'm at home in Europe. Working in other European countries for various designers has given me insights into the international fashion scene. Now I'd like to hand on this way of seeing things. This exhibition is one way of doing that.

You've just said 'objectivism is a lie'. I've got the impression that your choice is very strongly influenced by the designers' personalities and the way they have translated the Zeitgeist into design.

In Deutschland gibt es ein wunderbares Wort: „Modeschöpfer". Es geht also um Menschen, die zu Schöpfern werden. Der Schöpfer verkörpert den Geist in der Materie. Er gibt einer Idee, einer Inspiration eine äußere Form. Der Modeschöpfer greift Ideen und spirituelle Strömungen auf und legt sie den Menschen auf den Leib. Als zweite Haut sozusagen, als zeitgemäße äußere Hülle des Menschen.

Ist es aber für die meisten Menschen nicht eher egal, was sie tragen? Die greifen halt morgens in den Schrank und ziehen heraus, was gerade einigermaßen passt.

Egal wie ich mich kleide, ich sende damit Signale aus. Starke und unübersehbare Signale über meine Person. Wer sich nachlässig kleidet, sagt damit auch etwas aus. Es gibt keine Kleidung, die „stumm" ist. Kleidung ist eine nonverbale Kommunikationsform mit anderen Menschen. Ich kann nun selbst bestimmen, ob ich mir vorher überlege, welche Signale ich über mich aussenden möchte, und mit welcher Stimme ich kommunizieren möchte. Kommunikation ist immer da – ich will aber ganz bewusst bestimmen, was ich wie über mich mitteilen möchte. Modebewusstsein heißt nicht, irgendwelchen Trends hinterher zu rennen, sondern sich selbst ein Bewusstsein für sein eigenes Abbild zu schaffen, mit dem man in die Welt tritt.

Kannst du an einem Beispiel aus deiner Auswahl verdeutlichen, wie das Produkt, die Marke und der Designer verbunden sind?

Die Marke wird ja um eine Person, ein Gesicht aufgebaut. Es ist in einigen internationalen Häusern zu beobachten, dass sich neben dem Namen eines ehemaligen Modeschöpfers neue Namen und Gesichter finden. Dieser Trend ist bei Christian Dior deutlich erkennbar. Name und Produkt waren eins. Seit Anfang der 1990er Jahre wird das Haus Dior mit John Galliano ‚identifiziert'. Was bedeutet das? In Frankreich, Belgien, Italien, England und Japan ist es anerkannt, dass ein Modeschöpfer seine ganze Kreativität, Persönlichkeit und Identität in eine eigene Kollektion einfließen lässt. Auch in den USA ist das eine

In Germany there's a wonderful word: 'Modeschöpfer' – 'fashion creator'. So it concerns people who become creators. The creator embodies spirit in material. He gives an external form to an idea, an inspiration. The fashion creator picks up ideas and spiritual movements and puts them on people's bodies. As a second skin, so to speak, as a fittingly contemporary external wrapping for the human being.

But most people don't seem to care about what they're wearing, do they? They just grope into their wardrobe in the morning and pull out something that seems about right.

No matter how I dress I'm sending signals with my clothes. Strong, unmistakable signals about me as a person. If you dress scruffily, that says something too. There's no such thing as 'mute' clothing. Clothing is a non-verbal form of communication with other people. Now I can determine myself whether I'll think in advance about what signals I want to transmit about myself and the voice I want to communicate them with. Communication is always there – but I want to determine very consciously what I want to impart about myself. Fashion consciousness doesn't mean running after any old trends but rather creating consciousness in yourself of the image with which you appear in the world.

Can you, by taking an example from your choice, make clear how product, brand and designer are interlinked?

The brand is built up around a person, a face. You can observe in some international fashion houses that there are new names and faces apart from the name of some former couturier. This trend is clearly recognizable in Christian Dior. Name and product were identical. Since the early 1990s the House of Dior has been 'identified' with John Galliano. What does that mean? In France, Belgium, Italy, England and Japan they've realised that a fashion designer lets all his creativity, his whole personality and identity flow into a collection. And that is just as much a matter of course in the USA. In Germany, on the other hand, you have the perfect example of how German history has even left traces in fashion. Here the

Selbstverständlichkeit. In Deutschland hingegen kann man exemplarisch erkennen, wie die deutsche Geschichte auch in der Mode ihre Spuren hinterlässt. Hier steht die starke Persönlichkeit von Jil Sander mit ihrem Gesicht an vorderster Stelle. Obwohl sie überall präsent war, war es eher ihre stille Persönlichkeit, die einen diskreten und puren Stil prägte. Der Versuch, Persönlichkeit und Marke zu trennen (Jil Sander braucht keine Jil Sander, vgl. Pressekonferenz Prada 2001), ist gescheitert. Sander kehrte im Mai 2003 in ihr eigenes Haus zurück.

Du hast gesagt, die deutsche Geschichte hat hier ihre Spuren hinterlassen, wie meinst du das?

Alles, was mit Personenkult zu tun hat, mit der Emporhebung eines Menschen, das ist in Deutschland nur schwer möglich. Die deutsche Kultur will keine Stars, eher Bescheidenheit. Die totalitäre Vergangenheit, das schlechte Gewissen ganzer Generationen hat dazu beigetragen, dass die Verehrung von einzelnen Menschen immer einen üblen Beigeschmack hat.

Du selbst hast dich provokativ mit einem Satz von dieser Haltung distanziert, der immer wieder zitiert wird: „Ich habe keine Lust auf Demut – ich will gefeiert werden." Wie haben Menschen und Medien darauf und auf deine „Liebeserklärung an Deutschland" (so der Titel von Eva Gronbachs Kollektion 2002) reagiert?

Auf jeden Fall mit großer Aufmerksamkeit. Es scheint wirklich so zu sein, dass es in Deutschland ein Bedürfnis danach gibt, sich seiner Herkunft bewusst zu werden. Die Menschen verstehen nicht, warum alle Welt sich und ihre nationalen Errungenschaften feiert und nur wir Deutschen uns bescheiden sollen. Es geht darum, aufrecht und bewusst, mit Verantwortung und Freude am Leben die eigene Identität in der Welt zu vertreten. Die Reaktion der Medien war sehr positiv. Meine Kollektion 2002, die wir im Bonner Kanzleramt fotografiert haben, erhielt viel Aufmerksamkeit. Als dann auch noch der Musiksender MTV seine Moderatoren mit meiner Schwarz-Rot-Gold-Kollek-

strong personality of Jil Sander with her face is in the front ranks. Although she was in everything everywhere, it was her quiet personality that shaped a reticent and pure style. The attempt to separate personality from brand (Jil Sander doesn't need a Jil Sander, see the Prada press conference in 2001) failed. In May 2003 Sander went back to her own fashion house.

You said German history has left traces here; what do you mean by that?

Anything which has anything at all to do with the personality cult, with a person being elevated above others, is hardly possible in Germany. German culture doesn't like stars, if anything, it likes modesty. A totalitarian past, the bad conscience of entire generations, have contributed to giving veneration of individuals a nasty aftertaste.

You have distanced yourself provocatively from this stance with a sentence that keeps being quoted: 'I have no desire for humility – I want to be celebrated'. How have the public and the media reacted to your 'Declaration of Love to Germany' (the title of Eva Gronbach's 2002 collection)?

In any case with a great deal of attention. There really seems to be a need in Germany for becoming conscious of where we have come from. People just don't understand why everywhere else celebrates their achievements as nations and only we Germans are supposed to be modest. What's at stake here is representing our own identity in the world, with our heads up and consciously, with a sense of accountability and enjoying life. The media reaction was very positive. My 2002 collection, which we photographed in the Bonn Chancellery, attracted a lot of attention. When the music channel MTV dressed its presenters in my Black-Red-Gold Collection and the Federal Eagle, the subject was much discussed. Germany and Eva Gronbach are one note in a melody just as every country and every person are a note. I want this note to sound beautiful. Perhaps rather loud – that's OK too.

tion und dem Bundesadler ausgestattet hat, wurde das Thema gern und viel diskutiert. Deutschland und Eva Gronbach sind ein Ton in einer Melodie, so wie jedes Land und jeder Mensch ein Ton sind. Ich will, dass dieser Ton schön klingt. Vielleicht auch ein bisschen laut – das ist schon okay.

Kannst du einen Blick auf ein paar Exponate deiner Auswahl werfen und zeigen, wie Designer, Zeit und Nationalität sich beeinflussen und ausschlaggebend für die Gestalt der Mode sind?

Ich habe vorher schon von Jil Sander gesprochen. Als sie 1967 mit einem Laden anfing, wo sie andere Labels verkaufte, war in Deutschland Mode, mit der sich ein Designer vermarktet, nicht vorhanden. 1973 gab sie ihre erste Kollektion heraus. In der Kombination mit den Photographien von Peter Lindbergh entstand eine Stilprägung, in der immer Name, Gesicht und Mode eine Einheit bilden. Trotz dem großen, auch internationalen Erfolg blieb ihr Stil dennoch minimalistisch, fast puristisch und bescheiden. Nur mit diesen Tugenden war eine deutsche Modedesignerin für die Welt und für Deutschland akzeptabel.

Wie sieht es mit internationalen Designern aus. Gibt es da auch typische nationale Elemente, die dann weltweit getragen werden?

Ich habe beispielsweise Gianni Versace deshalb mit in die Auswahl aufgenommen, weil er mit seiner Mode das Glamouröse, Überladene und Luxuriöse in die Welt zurückgebracht hat. Seine italienische Herkunft, seine katholische Sozialisation, sein Frauenbild – alles findet sich in seiner sexy Silhouette wieder. Auf einmal ist die Welt ein Stück italienischer, antiker und üppiger. Gianni Versace und später seine Schwester Donatella haben ihr nationales und persönliches Statement auf einer neuen, überpersönlichen und übernationalen Ebene künstlerisch erneuert.

Can you take a look at some of your exhibits and show how designer, time and nationality influence each other and are crucial for the way fashion looks?

I've already mentioned Jil Sander. When she started out in 1967 with a shop where she sold other labels, there was no fashion branding in Germany to market a designer. In 1973 she launched her first collection. In combination with Peter Lindbergh's photography, a style was shaped in which name, face and fashion formed a unity. Despite her enormous success, abroad as well, her style nevertheless remained minimalist, almost purist and reticent. A German fashion designer could only be acceptable to the world and Germany with these virtues.

How do things as far as international designers are concerned? Are there typical national elements which are transmitted world-wide?

I chose Gianni Versace because he brought glamour, flamboyance, luxury back into the world with his fashions. His Italian origin, his Catholic socialization, his idea of women – all these things recur in his sexy silhouette. All of a sudden the world is a bit more Italian, more antique and more sumptuous. Gianni Versace and later his sister, Donatella, artistically renewed their national and personal commitment on a new, hyper-personal and transnational plane.

Aber nach diesem pompösen italienischen Stil scheint mir das Gegenteil davon erfolgreich gewesen zu sein. Ich finde es so typisch, dass auf die eine Bewegung eine ganz andere folgt. Ist das pures Kalkül, damit Mode immer weiter verkauft werden kann?

Würde Mode nur auf einem profanen und auf Profit orientierten Stilwechsel beruhen, würde niemand sie tragen. Mode funktioniert nur, weil sie auf realen Bedürfnissen basiert. Wenn man die Zeit nach Versaces großem Erfolg in den 1980er Jahren betrachtet, so traten die puren, schlichten, fließenden Ikonen, entworfen von Giorgio Armani und Jil Sander, wieder ans Licht. Oder schauen wir uns Vivienne Westwood an, die aus dem Land der Industrie, der Arbeit kommt. Westwood stellte sich gegen das britische Establishment und führte einen grundlegenden Wandel in der Art sich zu kleiden herbei. Sie nimmt die britische Gesellschaft als Inspiration und spiegelt diese mit Ironie und Witz. Eine Frau betrachtet das Potential einer Frau und kleidet diese in Kenntnis der europäischen Kostümgeschichte mit verschwenderischen Stoffen, die aber verfremdet werden. Eine Fülle neuer und schockierender Visionen gehen von Vivienne Westwood und ihrer Mode aus. Sie gab der Punkbewegung ein Outfit. „Destroy" stand auf dem T-Shirt, das sie 1976 entwarf.

Findet da nicht eine Vermischung von Politik und Mode statt, derer du dich auch in deiner Deutschland-Kollektion bedienst?

Ja, seit Westwood konnten Politik und Mode verknüpft werden. Nationale Elemente wie Farben und Hoheitszeichen werden ironisch benutzt und künstlerisch verfremdet. Dies ist auch die Arbeitsweise von John Galliano. Er liebt ebenfalls die Inszenierung und Übertreibung. Auch er bedient sich der Historie.

Es gibt ja in vielen Ländern nationale Farben und Symbole, die als chic gelten.

Klar, bis auf Deutschland – aus verständlichen Gründen. Mit der Kol-

But after that bombastic Italian style the opposite seems to me to have been successful. I find it so typical that a movement is followed by an entirely different one. Is that calculated so that fashions can keep on being sold?

If fashions just rested on a profane change in style with a view to profits, no one would wear them. Fashion only functions when it's based on real needs. When you look at the time after Versace's big success in the 1980s, the pure, simple, flowing icons designed by Giorgio Armani and Jil Sander again come into the light of day. Or just look at Vivienne Westwood, who comes from the land of industry, of work. Westwood opposed the British establishment and has caused fundamental change in the way people dress. She lets herself be inspired by British society and reflects it with irony and wit. A woman looks at a woman's potential and dresses her in full awareness of the history of European costume in lavish fabrics which have been given a dose of the alienation effect. A wealth of new and shocking visions emanate from Vivienne Westwood and her fashion. She outfitted the Punk movement. 'Destroy' is written on a T-shirt she designed in 1976.

Isn't a blending of politics and fashion taking place there that you also use in your Germany Collection?

Yes, since Westwood it's been possible to link politics and fashion. National elements such as colours and insignia are used ironically and treated to an artistic alienation effect. That's also John Galliano's approach. He also loves staginess and exaggeration. He, too, makes use of history.

There are national colours and symbols in many countries which are regarded as chic.

lektion „Liebeserklärung an Deutschland" ist deshalb ein Tabubruch auf zwei Ebenen vollzogen worden: politisch, weil eine neue Generation von Deutschen sich mit Farben und Symbolen schmückt, die für alles stehen, nur nicht für spaßige Unbekümmertheit und Weltoffenheit. Aber auch in der Ästhetik ereignete sich ein Bruch, da die deutschen Nationalfarben bisher als hässlich galten. Es ist unheimlich spannend zu sehen, wie sich die Wahrnehmung ändert: Hässliches wird schön, allein durch die Art, wie man es betrachtet. Mode hat hier die Sicht auf die Welt verändert.

Wir haben über Politik und Gesellschaft als Inspiration gesprochen, was gibt es noch für Quellen, aus denen ein Modedesigner schöpfen kann? Welche Umbildung von Werten gibt es sonst noch, die du in deiner Auswahl berücksichtigt hast?

Der Einsatz der UNO-Truppen in Ex-Jugoslawien hat das Bild des Soldaten verändert. Dort war der Soldat als humanitärer Retter im Einsatz. Er wurde zum Idol. Danach tauchten überall Elemente auf, die aus dem militärischen Bereich übernommen wurden. Der Military-Look mit den Camouflage-Prints in sämtlichen olivgrünen Tönen gehört zum aktuellen Straßenbild und ist von Designern wie Elternhaus® Maegde u. Knechte® bis hin zu Comme des Garçons interpretiert worden.

Wenn du von neuen Ikonen sprichst, dann fällt mir noch der Sportler ein. Wie kannst du sportliche Aspekte einordnen?

Der Sportler ist ein Held. Er ist bereit, über sich hinauszuwachsen. Sein Ziel ist nicht materieller Natur. Es geht darum, Ziele zu erreichen, ohne dass hiermit ein materielles Ergebnis verbunden wäre. Das ist im Grunde der pure Idealismus. Der Turnschuh oder Sneaker ist als Schuhwerk nicht mehr wegzudenken. Firmen wie Adidas und Puma sind absolute Kultfirmen. Adidas ist seit 2002 eine Kooperation mit Yohji Yamamoto eingegangen. Es entsteht nun die Kollektion Y-3, womit Yamamotos Modehandschrift auf einem Sportlabel erscheint.

132–134 Aline, Xenia und Hodan im Bonner Kanzleramt / Aline, Xenia and Hodan at the Bonn Chancellery
Eva Gronbach, 2002

Definitely, except in Germany – for understandable reasons. 'A Declaration of Love to Germany' therefore represents a break with taboos on two planes: politically, because a new generation of Germans are adorning themselves with colours and symbols which stand for anything but fun and casualness and receptiveness to the world. But an aesthetic break has also occurred since the German national colours have been regarded as ugly up to now. It's awfully exciting to see how perceptions are changing: what was ugly is becoming beautiful, just in the way it's looked at. Here fashion has changed the way the world is viewed.

We've talked about politics and society as inspiration; what other sources are there for a fashion designer to draw on? What other value modifications are there which you have taken into account in making your selection?

The deployment of UN troops in former Yugoslavia has changed the image of the soldier. There soldiers were deployed as humanitarian rescuers. They became idols. Afterwards elements surfaced everywhere which had been taken over from the military. The Military Look with camouflage prints in all shades of olive green is part and parcel of the current street scene and has been interpreted by designers such as Elternhaus® Maegde u. Knechte® on up to Comme des Garçons.

When you talk of new icons, I also think of athletes. How do you classify sporting aspects?

The sportsman is a hero. He's willing to transcend himself. His goals are not material in nature. What's at stake is attaining goals without a material result being linked with them. That is basically idealism pure and simple. Life is now unthinkable without trainers or sneakers on your feet. Firms like Adidas and Puma are absolutely cult. Adidas has been collaborating with Yohji Yamamoto since 2002. Now a Y-3 Collection is being created with Yamamoto's fashion signature on a sporting label. Here, too, what used to be fusty old sports clothing is now regarded as hip because a reinterpretation of the symbols has taken place. To me real highlights are when it's possible to change the idea and not the object itself.

Auch hier gilt nun ehemals muffige Sportbekleidung als hip, weil eine Umdeutung der Symbole stattgefunden hat. Für mich sind das wirkliche Highlights, wenn es gelingt, die Idee zu verändern und nicht den Gegenstand selbst.

Kannst du diese Umdeutung von Symbolen noch an anderen Beispielen aus den letzten Jahren veranschaulichen? Ich habe das Gefühl, dass es hier um eine wesentliche Entwicklung geht.

Die ganze Hip-Hop-Mode mit den Hosen, die in den Kniekehlen hängen, ist aus der Umdeutung von Symbolen entstanden. In den amerikanischen Gefängnissen wurden ethnischen Minderheiten die Gürtel weggenommen. Dies geschah einerseits, um der Suizidgefahr vorzubeugen, andererseits, um die Insassen zu entwürdigen. Aus Solidarität zogen die Sänger und Rapper auf der Bühne ebenfalls ihre Gürtel aus. Plötzlich war aus einer Hose, die Demütigung darstellen sollte, ein Zeichen des Stolzes und der Solidarität geworden.

Dieser Hip-Hop-Style aus den USA ist zu einer internationalen Bewegung geworden. Wir haben über Deutschland, Europa und die USA gesprochen. Welche Einflüsse hast du aus der asiatischen Welt mit in deine Auswahl genommen?

Die Japaner haben zu Beginn der 1980er Jahre einen Austausch der Kulturen bewirkt. Die Präsenz der Japaner Issey Miyake, Yohji Yamamoto und Rei Kawakubo in Paris hat zunächst einen Schock und dann eine Welle der Kreativität ausgelöst. Von diesem Eindruck inspiriert, startete eine neue Mode-Bewegung in Belgien. Mit Linda Loppa an der Spitze wurde die Akademie in Antwerpen zum Zentrum der Kreativität. Authentizität ist das Zauberwort, welches dort gelehrt wird. Der persönliche und individuelle Ausdruck ist das Entscheidende. Dafür stehen Martin Margiela, Ann Demeulemeester, Dries van Noten, Walter van Beirendonck, jeder mit seiner ganz eigenen Aussage.

Das sind alles Belgier. Ist deren Einfluss wirklich so prägend für das internationale Modegeschehen?

Can you illustrate that reinterpretation of symbols with some more examples from recent years? I've got the feeling that what's at stake here is an essential development.

The whole hip-hop fashion with baggy pants hanging around your knees has arisen from the reinterpretation of symbols. In American prisons, belts are taken away from ethnic minorities. This has been done, on the one hand, to prevent the danger of suicide but, on the other, to demean inmates. Singers and Rappers showed their solidarity by also taking off their belts on stage. Suddenly a pair of pants that was supposed to represent humiliation had become a sign of pride and solidarity.

This hip-hop style from the US has become an international movement. We've talked about Germany, Europe and the US. What influences from Asia have you taken into account in your selection?

The Japanese sparked off a cultural exchange in the 1980s. The presence of the Japanese Issey Miyake, Yohji Yamamoto and Rei Kawakubo in Paris at first caused a shock and then released a wave of creativity. Inspired by this impression, a new fashion movement started in Belgium. Spearheaded by Linda Loppa, the Antwerp Academy became a hive of creativity. Authenticity is the magic word that's taught there. Personal, individual expression is what counts. That's what Martin Margiela, Ann Demeulemeester, Dries van Noten, Walter van Beirendonck all stand for, each with their own distinctive statement.

They are all Belgians. Do they really exert such a formative influence on what happens on the international fashion scene?

Ja. Das belgische Selbstbewusstsein in der Mode bringt eine ganz neue Bewegung in das internationale Modegeschehen. Die „Groupe des Six" zeigte Anfang der 1980er Jahre erstmals ihre Kollektionen in London und in Paris und erregt nun schon seit bald zwanzig Jahren Aufsehen. Am Anfang der Bewegung stand das rohe, harte flämische Bewusstsein, das im verspielten, zarten, oberflächlichen Paris zu schock-ähnlichen Begegnungen führte. Die Akademie in Antwerpen bekam jedoch immer mehr internationalen Zulauf. In der Nachfolge konnte sich eine deutsche Gruppe etablieren. Hierfür stehen Namen wie Bernhard Willhelm und Stephan Schneider. Seit Mitte der 1990er Jahre steht die Brüsseler Akademie La Cambre international sowie innerhalb Belgiens für eine neue Bewegung. Hier wurden unter anderem Olivier Theyskens (Rochas) und Jose Ons Selfa (Leowe) ausgebildet.

Eva, wir haben jetzt nur einige wenige Dinge angesprochen. Könntest du am Ende in ein paar Worten deine Auswahl beschreiben und begründen – und eine Aussicht geben auf das, was kommt?

Wichtig ist mir, dem Betrachter einen internationalen Überblick zu geben. In der Mode findet schon immer ein Kulturaustausch statt. Zudem geht es darum, die Unterschiede der Designer-Persönlichkeiten zu verdeutlichen. Jeder Designer spricht eine eigene und zugleich extreme Sprache. Extreme sind notwendig, um klare Aussagen finden zu können. Mancher Betrachter wird sich denken, dass man die Kleider in der Ausstellung nicht täglich tragen kann, da sie zu „ausgeflippt" erscheinen mögen. Meine Antwort darauf lautet: Ja, aber die Aussagen der Exponate sind fühlbar. Als Ausblick biete ich dem Betrachter eine Auswahl junger deutscher Designer, die momentan international viel Aufmerksamkeit bekommen. Diese Designer leben nicht nur in Deutschland, sondern auch in London, Paris oder Antwerpen. Alle haben eines gemeinsam: Sie treten mit ihrer deutschen Identität auf, und diese fließt auf unterschiedlichste Art in ihre Arbeit ein. Ich denke, wir stehen heute erst am Anfang einer neuen Bewegung.

Das Gespräch mit Eva Gronbach führte ihr Bruder Sebastian Gronbach (Journalist).

Yes. Belgian fashion self-confidence has brought an entirely new movement into the international fashion scene. The 'Groupe des Six' first showed collections in London and Paris in the early 1980s and they've been attracting attention for nearly twenty years now. The movement originated in the rough, tough Flemish consciousness which made a shocking impact on playful, exquisite, superficial Paris. The Antwerp Academy, however, has become increasingly popular world-wide. A German group has subsequently been able to establish itself. It's represented by such names as Bernhard Willhelm and Stephan Schneider. Since the mid-1990s the La Cambre Academy in Brussels has represented a new movement, both within Belgium and abroad. That's where Olivier Theyskens (Rochas) and Jose Ons Selfa (Leowe), among others, trained.

Eva, we've only touched on a few things up to now. Could you close by describing your selection in a few words and justifying it – and give us some idea of what is forthcoming?

What's important to me is to give viewers an international survey. Cultural exchange has always taken place in fashion. Moreover, I'm concerned with highlighting the differences between the various designers. Each designer speaks a distinctive and also extreme language. Extremes are necessary for arriving at unequivocal statements. Some viewers will think that the clothes in the show aren't for everyday wear because they may seem so 'off the wall'. My answer to that is: Yes, but the statements made by the exhibits are palpable. The prospect I'm offering viewers is a selection of young German designers who are attracting a great deal of attention world-wide at the moment. These designers don't just live in Germany. They also live in London, Paris or Antwerp. What they have in common is they stand up for their identity as Germans and this stance informs their work in the most diverse ways. I think today we're on the brink of a new movement.

The interview with Eva Gronbach was conducted by her brother, Sebastian Gronbach (journalist).

Die Mode ist weiblichen Geschlechts, hat folglich ihre Launen.
Fashion is feminine and, therefore, capricious.

Nachwort

Gerhard Dietrich

Nicht was schön ist, ist Mode, sondern was Mode ist, ist schön.
(Sprichwörtliche Redensart)

Die Mode ist weiblichen Geschlechts, hat folglich ihre Launen.
(K. J. Weber, Demokritos 8,6: Die Satire der Neueren, aus: Zoozmanns
Zitatenschatz der Weltliteratur, Leipzig 1919, Sp. 831)

135 Stephen Jones, „Bird"
London, 2003

Mode ist ein vitaler Bereich unserer Kultur und Identität, ob man sich
nun dessen bewusst ist oder nicht. Unsere Kleiderwahl offenbart sehr
viel über das eigene Selbstverständnis und letztlich auch über das Bild,
das wir den anderen über uns vermitteln möchten. Mode besteht zu
einem nicht geringen Teil aus Wahrnehmung, persönlichem Geschmack
und Stilgefühl. Unter Mode versteht man aber auch bewusst entwickelte und spätestens seit 1800 in sämtlichen verfügbaren Medien
gezielt propagierte saisonale Trends, die den wechselhaften gesellschaftlichen Konformitätszwängen entsprechend Züge eines allgemein
verbindlichen Modediktats annehmen können. Nicht erst heute ziehen
wir uns je nach Anlass und eigenem Befinden mehrmals täglich an und
aus, kleiden uns, um erfolgreich zu sein, um zu beeindrucken, um zu
entspannen. Stets treffen wir eine Aussage über uns selbst, mit jedem
Knopf, mit jedem Reißverschluss, mit jedem Muster und jeder Silhouette. Mode kann den Körper schmücken, ihm Bedeutung und Macht
verleihen, ihm zu sozialem Ansehen verhelfen, ihn begehrenswert und
schön erscheinen lassen. Die übergezogene zweite Haut schützt vor
Wind, Wetter und gesellschaftlich nicht tolerierter Nacktheit, demons-
triert, suggeriert oder postuliert aber auch – Kleider machen Leute
– eine soziale, durchaus wandelbare Gruppenzugehörigkeit und kodi-
fiziert die öffentliche und private Sphäre jedes Einzelnen. Mode ist
ein vielseitiges Medium und vielschichtiges Phänomen mit zahlreichen
Funktionen, sozialen und symbolischen Bedeutungsebenen, die es zu
kennen, zu beachten und zu nutzen gilt. Nicht zuletzt ist Mode kurzle-
big, häufig ein Luxusgeschäft des schönen und vergänglichen Scheins,
das sich in einem schier unendlichen Reichtum von Schöpfungen unab-
lässig wandelt und sich doch zyklisch zu wiederholen scheint.

Afterthoughts

Gerhard Dietrich

Fashion is not what is beautiful but what is fashionable is beautiful.
(Proverb)

Fashion is feminine and, therefore, capricious.
(K. J. Weber, Demokritos 8,6: Die Satire der Neueren, from: Zoozmanns Zitatenschatz der Weltliteratur, Leipzig 1919, col. 831)

Fashion is a crucial area of our culture and our identity whether we are aware of this or not. Our choice of clothes reveals a great deal about our self-image and ultimately about the image of ourselves we would like to convey to others. Fashion consists to a great extent in perception, personal taste and stylishness. What is meant by fashion is also deliberately developed and, at the latest since 1800, seasonal trends disseminated in all available media, trends which can assume the characteristics of a universally binding fashion diktat matching the vagaries of societal constraints to conform. We are not the first generation to change our clothes several times a day depending on the occasion and how we feel, to be successful, to make an impression and simply to relax. In so doing, we invariably make a statement about ourselves with each button, zip, pattern and silhouette. Fashion can adorn the body, lend it significance and power, help it to achieve social status and make it appear desirable and beautiful. The second skin we pull on over the first one protects us from wind, weather and nakedness, which is not sanctioned by society, suggesting or positing belongingness, even though this may change, to a social group – clothes maketh the man – and codifying both the public and the private life of each and every one of us. Fashion is a versatile medium, a complex phenomenon with numerous functions, societal and symbolic planes of meaning which one must know, observe and exploit. Not least are fashions short-lived, often a luxury trade in beauty and the transience of appearances which is continually changing in a limitless wealth of creations yet seems to recur on a cyclical basis.

Mode für Frauen ist von jeher mit dem Streben nach Schönheit, Eleganz und Raffinesse verbunden. In ihr kommen das Kapriziöse und Kokette, das Extravagante und vor allem das Erotische zum Ausdruck. Sie verhüllt und verbirgt die Körperformen oftmals nur, um sie umso deutlicher zu offenbaren. Mode für Frauen, nicht selten von Männern entworfen, weckt vielfach und oft nichts weniger als absichtsvoll das Begehren von Männern. Zu diesem Zweck kann sie den Körper, den sie um- und enthüllt, auf überraschend vielfältige Art modellieren, in seinen Reizpotentialen betonen, ungeachtet der anatomischen Voraussetzungen gewaltsam deformieren oder grotesk überformen. Je nach geltendem Schönheitsideal wirkt ein solchermaßen geschmückter oder geschundener Leib dann ganz besonders aufreizend.

Mit diesem schon seit der Antike stets im Vordergrund stehenden Themenkomplex der Mode, der Modellierung des Weiblichen, setzen sich das vorliegende Werk – und die gleichnamige Ausstellung – auseinander. Dabei dokumentieren repräsentative Kostümentwürfe aus dem Besitz des Museums für Angewandte Kunst Köln sowie Leihgaben namhafter europäischer Modeschöpfer der Gegenwart exemplarisch die oft erst durch die Mode definierten Schönheitsideale und deren Ausformung in der weiblichen Kontur. Buch und Ausstellung präsentieren ausgesuchte Beispiele aus charakteristischen Epochen wie Klassizismus, Empire oder Biedermeier und lenken den Blick des Betrachters auf das jeweils modische Erscheinungsbild der Dame in Europa. Ziel war es dabei natürlich nicht allein, grundlegende Entwicklungsmuster der Modegeschichte unter dem Aspekt des gewählten Themas bis in die Gegenwart hinein zu verdeutlichen, das Verhältnis von weiblichem Körper und seinem Kleid generell in seiner zeitlichen Bedingtheit und modischer Wandelbarkeit nachvollziehbar zu machen. Ziel war es nicht zuletzt, den großen Reichtum des modeschöpfenden Menschen an gestalterischer Raffinesse, an ästhetischem Empfinden, an erotischer Imagination, an innovativer Potenz, an kunsthandwerklicher Virtuosität und Perfektion sowie an künstlerischer Inspiration erfahrbar zu machen, der in der Mode der Vergangenheit und der Gegenwart zu bestaunen ist. Dieser Reichtum ist ungebrochen lebendig: Vor allem

136 Stephen Jones, „Snowstrobe"
London, 2003

Ladies' fashions have been associated from time immemorial with a striving for beauty, elegance and sophistication. Fashion expresses caprice and coquetry, extravagance and above all eroticism. It disguises and conceals body shapes, often only to disclose them all the more revealingly. Women's fashions, so often designed by men, frequently arouse men's lust and this is often deliberate. To this end it can modulate the body it at once wraps up and discloses in a surprising variety of ways by emphasizing its stimulus potential regardless of underlying anatomical conditions, by either brutally deforming it or grotesquely reshaping it. A body thus adorned or maltreated appears particularly provocative depending on the ideal of beauty prevailing at a given time.

The present book – and the exhibition of the same name – deals with the shaping of femininity via the thematic complex that is fashion, one that has remained a focus of interest since antiquity. In both book and exhibition, representative costume designs owned by the Museum of Applied Art Cologne as well as silhouettes loaned by distinguished contemporary European fashion designers exemplify ideals of beauty, so often defined by fashion, and the impact they have had on the styling of feminine contours. Both the present book and the exhibition present a selection exemplifying such characteristic period styles as Neo-Classicism, Empire and German Biedermeier, directing the viewer's eye to what made a lady appear stylish in Europe in each of those eras. The aim was, of course, not just to elucidate thematically basic developmental patterns in the history of fashion on into the present but also to trace the relationship of the female body to dress in general with all its temporal limitations and the mutability of fashion. The aim was also and not least to make it possible to experience the enormous wealth of sophistication in design, the aesthetic sense, the erotic imagination, the potential for innovation, the virtuosity of consummate craftsmanship and ultimately the artistic inspiration drawn on by those who create fashion, all qualities which were admirable in the past and still evoke astonishment today. This wealth is still as alive as ever: in the work of many young contemporary fashion designers especially a new, significant stance is strikingly apparent: fashion is being increasingly regarded as an art form which exacts of its

in den Arbeiten vieler jüngerer zeitgenössischer Modedesigner ist eine neue signifikante Haltung spürbar: Mode wird zunehmend als Kunstform betrachtet, die ein hohes Maß an bildnerischer Ausdruckskraft und schöpferischem Einfühlungsvermögen in die heutige Zeit erfordert. Designer agieren nicht mehr nur auf dem Laufsteg, sondern formen Körperkonstrukte, die an der Schnittstelle zu bildnerischen Werken stehen und die Vielseitigkeit der zeitgenössischen Modeszene bezeugen.

137 Stephen Jones, „Myth"
London, 2003

Idee und Konzeption von Ausstellung und Publikation entwickelte hochmotiviert und engagiert die Leiterin der Modesammlung am Museum für Angewandte Kunst Köln, Patricia Brattig. In ihren Händen lagen Organisation und Durchführung des Gesamtprojekts. Sie kuratierte den Überblick über rund 220 Jahre europäischer Modegeschichte, der sich aus dem Bestand des Museums selbst speist und zahlreiche bedeutende Neuerwerbungen erstmals der Öffentlichkeit präsentiert. Somit spiegeln Ausstellung und Publikation auch die Großzügigkeit der dem Museum verbundenen Mäzene, Stifter und Sammler, Freunde und Förderer sowie Bürger der Stadt Köln, aus deren Privatbesitz viele Kostüme stammen und denen an dieser Stelle unser tief empfundener Dank gebührt. Für den komplementären Ausstellungsteil mit den Kreationen gefeierter Modeschöpfer und vielversprechender, noch nicht etablierter Designer konnte die junge aufstrebende Modedesignerin Eva Gronbach als Gastkuratorin gewonnen werden. Die ausgebildete Schneiderin studierte Modedesign in Paris und Brüssel und perfektionierte ihr Talent bei Yohji Yamamoto, John Galliano und Hermès. Aufsehen erregte ihre erste eigene Kollektion „Liebeserklärung an Deutschland" (2002). Leitmotiv für Eva Gronbachs Auswahl war ebenfalls die Auseinandersetzung mit dem weiblichen Körper, seiner Modellierung oder gar auch Entkörperlichung mit den Mitteln der Mode. Unter den gewährten Leihgaben befinden sich viele Inkunabeln der modernen und jüngsten Modegeschichte.

practitioners a high degree of visual prowess and creative empathy in today's world. Designers no longer operate only on the catwalk. They also mould body constructs which are at the interface between the applied and the fine arts, attesting to the versatility of the contemporary fashion scene.

The idea and conception of both the exhibition and the book were developed by Patricia Brattig, head curator of the fashion collection at the Museum of Applied Art Cologne, with unflagging enthusiasm and unstinting commitment. She was responsible for organising and carrying out the entire project. As curator she oversaw a sweeping survey of two hundred and twenty years of European fashion history, drawing on the Museum collection and presenting numerous major recent acquisitions for the first time to the public. Consequently, both the exhibition and the present book reflect the generosity of patrons of the Museum, donors and collectors, friends and promoters as well as the people of the city of Cologne, from whose private collections many costumes came. To them we owe first of all heartfelt thanks. The dynamic young designer Eva Gronbach graciously consented as guest curator to take charge of the complementary part of the exhibition, featuring the creations of celebrated couturiers and promising designers who are not yet part of the fashion establishment. After training as a sempstress, she studied fashion design in Paris and Brussels, honing her talent to perfection by studying with Yohji Yamamoto, John Galliano and Hermès. Her first collection, 'A Declaration of Love to Germany' (2002), created a sensation. Eva Gronbach was guided in her choice of exhibits by the theme of the female body, how it is shaped or even dematerialised by means of fashion. Among the exhibits on loan are numerous incunabula of modern and contemporary fashion history. For their willingness to part for the duration of the exhibition from their precious silhouettes and catwalk photographs and place them at the disposal of this publication we are indebted to renowned houses of haute couture from all over Europe.

Für die Bereitschaft der renommierten Haute Couture-Häuser aus ganz Europa, sich für die Dauer der Ausstellung von ihren wertvollen Silhouetten zu trennen und Laufstegaufnahmen für die Publikation zur Verfügung zu stellen, danken wir sehr.

Die Ausstellungsinszenierung konzipierte der Kölner Architekt Uwe Bernd Friedemann. Von 1991 bis 2000 war er bei Peter Kulka in Köln und Dresden tätig. Er betreute u.a. von 1991 bis 1993 den Neubau des Sächsischen Landtags in Dresden und nahm an zahlreichen erstplatzierten Wettbewerben teil. Seit 1996 widmet er sich selbständigen Planungen. In zahlreichen Gesprächen und Sitzungen mit den Ausstellungsplanern gelangte Uwe Bernd Friedemann zu einer klaren, reduzierten Architektur, die allen beteiligten Modeschöpfern gleichermaßen gerecht wird und vor allem den Exponaten den Vorrang belässt.

Wir danken den Mitarbeitern des Verlages Arnoldsche Art Publishers, insbesondere dem geschäftsführenden Gesellschafter Dieter Zühlsdorff, dafür, dass sie diese Publikation in das Verlagsprogramm aufgenommen haben. Die zweisprachige Ausgabe in Deutsch und Englisch beruht auf der Initiative des Verlegers, dessen kenntnisreiche Betreuung und besondere Sorgfalt bei der Drucklegung des Kataloges in dem reich bebilderten, handlichen Buch deutlich zum Tragen kommt. Die graphische Gestaltung und das Layout des Kataloges übernahm mit großer Begeisterung, ungebremstem Eifer und Ideenreichtum die junge Graphik-Designerin Kristine Klein aus Köln. Die Neuaufnahmen der Kostüme aus dem Bestand des Museums für Angewandte Kunst Köln besorgte Anna C. Wagner vom Rheinischen Bildarchiv, assistiert von Nicole Cronauge. Die Scherenschnitte, die die Silhouetten der historischen Kostüme mit den für das Verständnis so wichtigen Elementen wie Frisuren, Kopfbedeckungen und Accessoires vervollständigen, stammen aus der talentierten Hand von Akiko Bernhöft.

138 Stephen Jones, „Striking"
London, 2003

The Cologne architect Uwe Bernd Friedemann designed the exhibition. From 1991 until 2000 he worked for Peter Kulka in Cologne and Dresden. One of his projects was overseeing the rebuilding of the Saxon State Parliament in Dresden from 1991 until 1993. He has participated in numerous competitions in which he as been awarded first place. Since 1996 he has been a self-employed architect. In countless conversations and discussion sessions with the planners of the exhibition, Uwe Bernd Friedemann arrived at stringent architecture, stripped of non-essentials, which does justice to all fashion designers participating and leaves centre stage to the exhibits themselves.

We wish to thank everyone at our publishers, Arnoldsche Art Publishers, especially managing director Dieter Zühlsdorff, for taking this publication into their programme. The book is published in German and English at the suggestion of the publisher, whose knowledgeable supervision and meticulous care are manifest in the printing of the catalogue in a book so lavishly illustrated and conveniently arranged. The graphic design and layout of the catalogue are the work of the young graphic designer Kristine Klein in Cologne, who took on this task with boundless enthusiasm and imagination. The new photographs of costumes from the Museum of Applied Art Cologne have been provided by Anna C. Wagner of the Rheinisches Bildarchiv, assisted by Nicole Cronauge. The silhouettes, cut outs of historical costume so essential to rounding off our knowledge of such important aspects as hairstyles, head-gear and accessories, are from the talented hand of Akiko Bernhöft.

An dieser Stelle gebührt vor allem den Autorinnen der Katalog-
beiträge besonderer Dank, die in ihren Texten interdisziplinär Teil-
aspekte zur Entstehung und Ausformung von Weiblichkeitsbildern in
der Gesellschaft und deren Vermittlung und Verbreitung durch die
Mode erkunden. Dabei fügen sich die von verschiedenen Fachberei-
chen beleuchteten Facetten zu einem geschlossen wahrnehmbaren
Begriff der modischen Frau zu verschiedenen Zeiten zusammen.

139 Stephen Jones, „Emperor"
London, 2003

Eine großzügige und verständnisvolle Unterstützung wurde uns bei
diesem Ausstellungsprojekt – wie so oft – von den Förderern des
Museums für Angewandte Kunst Köln, der Overstolzengesellschaft,
zuteil, die die Kosten für die Drucklegung der Museumsausgabe des
Begleitbuches vertrauensvoll vorfinanzierten. Zum Erfolg der Ausstellung haben aber darüber hinaus nicht zuletzt auch die mit ihrem Logo
in dieser Publikation vertretenen Sponsoren maßgeblich beigetragen,
insbesondere die Stadtsparkasse Köln, der wir uns zutiefst verpflichtet
fühlen. Allen Sponsoren und Mäzenen, ohne deren Hilfe dieses Projekt
nicht zustande gekommen wäre, gebührt unser ausdrücklicher, tief
empfundener Dank.

At this juncture we should especially like to thank the authors of the catalogue essays, who explore aspects of the creation and development of ideas of femininity in their social context and their transmission and dissemination through fashion in an interdisciplinary approach. It fits together the various specialist disciplines to form a complete perception of what it meant to be a stylish lady at different times in history.

We were supported and with great generosity and empathy in this exhibition project – as we have been so many times before – by the promoters of the Museum of Applied Art Cologne, the Overstolzengesellschaft, who without hesitation assumed the cost of having the Museum edition of the book printed. Moreover, the sponsors whose logos appear in this publication have made a vital contribution to the success of the exhibition, especially the Stadtsparkasse Köln, to whom we owe a great debt of gratitude. We should like to express our heartfelt thanks to all our sponsors ans patrons without whose help this project could not have been realised.

Die Autorinnen

Uta Brandes (geb. 1949)

Designtheoretikerin (Dr. phil.). Studierte Anglistik, Politische Wissenschaften, Soziologie und Psychologie in Hannover. Promovierte 1983. Stellvertretende Leiterin des Forschungsinstitutes „Frau und Gesellschaft" in Hannover. Leitende Ministerialrätin und Abteilungsleiterin bei der hessischen Bevollmächtigten für Frauenangelegenheiten. 1990–92 Konzeption des Schweizer Design Center in Langenthal. 1992–94 Direktorin des „Forum" der Kunst- und Ausstellungshalle der Bundesrepublik Deutschland in Bonn. Seit 1995 Professorin für Gender und Design sowie für qualitative Designforschung an der Köln International School of Design. 1. Vorsitzende der Deutschen Gesellschaft für Designtheorie und -forschung (DGTF). Forschungsschwerpunkte: genderspezifisches Design; Geschlecht – Körper, vergeschlechtlichte Produkte; neue Formen empirischer Designforschung.

Luzie Bratner (geb. 1969)

Kunsthistorikerin (Dr. phil.). Studierte Kunstgeschichte, Klassische Archäologie und Italienisch in Mainz und Wien. Promotion zur deutschen Sepulkralskulptur des 17. und 18. Jahrhunderts. Seit 2000 am Museum für Angewandte Kunst Köln tätig. Forschungsschwerpunkt: europäische Malerei und Bildhauerei des Barock und Rokoko.

Patricia Brattig (geb. 1968)

Kunsthistorikerin (Dr. phil.). Studierte Kunstgeschichte, Romanische Philologie und Klassische Archäologie in Köln und Paris. Promovierte 1998 über das „Schloss von Vaux-le-Vicomte". Seit 1998 am Museum für Angewandte Kunst Köln tätig, seit 2000 als Leiterin der Mode- und Textilabteilung sowie der Glas- und Keramikabteilung. Forschungsschwerpunkte: französische Architektur und Innendekoration des 17. und 18. Jahrhunderts; Modegeschichte; Tapisserien.

Karen Ellwanger (geb. 1953)

Kulturwissenschaftlerin (Prof. Dr. phil.). Studierte Empirische Kulturwissenschaft, Allgemeine Rhetorik und Soziologie in Tübingen und Vergleichende Textilwissenschaft in Dortmund. Promovierte 1994 zum Thema „Bekleidung im Modernisierungsprozess 1870–1930. Frauen, Mode, Mobilität". Seit 1982 Lehr- und Forschungstätigkeit an verschiedenen Universitäten (Tübingen, Osnabrück, Ulm, Göttingen, Dortmund, Solothurn) und der Hochschule der Künste in Berlin. Seit 1994 Professorin für Kulturgeschichte europäischer Textilien an der Carl von Ossietzky Universität in Oldenburg, seit 2003 am Kulturwissenschaftlichen Institut „Kunst-Textil-Medien". Sprecherin des Kollegs/Promotionsstudiengangs „Kulturwissenschaftliche Geschlechterstudien". Forschungsschwerpunkte: Kleidung und Körperbild in der Moderne; vestimentäre Repräsentationen des Politischen; empirische Lebensstilforschung.

Elke Gaugele (geb. 1964)

Empirische Kulturwissenschaftlerin (Dr. phil.). Studierte Europäische Ethnologie, Geschichte und Politikwissenschaften in Berlin, Tübingen und Wien. Mehrjährige Berufstätigkeit als Kuratorin. Promovierte 1999 über die „Kleidung als Medium der Genderkonstruktion". Derzeit habilitiert sie als Wissenschaftliche Assistentin am Institut für Kunst und Kunsttheorie, Abteilung Textil der Universität zu Köln. Fellowship am Goldsmith College, London (2003/2004) und Maria-Goeppert-Mayer Gastprofessur für internationale Genderforschung (2004). Forschungsschwerpunkte: Genderkonstruktion an der Schnittstelle von Körper und Kleidung; Mode, Konsum und visuelle Kultur; Feldforschung und performative Verfahren.

Eva Gronbach (geb. 1971)

Modedesignerin. Absolvierte nach dem Abitur eine Lehre als Damenschneiderin in Düsseldorf, 1995 Gesellenbrief. 1995 bis 2000 Diplomstudiengang „Stylisme et Création de la Mode" am Institut supérieur des arts visuels La Cambre in Brüssel. 1997 Praktikantin bei Stephen Jones in London. 1998 Erasmus-Austausch am Institut français de la Mode in Paris (Abschluss: „European Master of Art"). 1999 Praktikum bei Yohji Yamamoto in Paris. Arbeitete für die Häuser John Galliano und Hermès. Seit 2000 als eigenständige Modedesignerin in Köln tätig.

Ingrid Heimann (geb. 1934)

Kunsthistorikerin (Prof. Dr. phil.). Studierte Kunstpädagogik an der Staatlichen Hochschule für Bildende Künste Berlin sowie Kunstgeschichte, Mathematik und Informationswissenschaft an der Technischen Universität Berlin. 1963 Assessorin des Lehramts. 1972 Professorin für Designtheorie an der Hochschule der Künste Berlin. Forschungsschwerpunkt: Bekleidungsformalität.

The Authors

Uta Brandes (b. 1949)

Design theorist (Dr. phil.). Studied English language and literature, political science, sociology and psychology in Hannover. Doctorate in 1983. Deputy of the institute 'Woman and Society' in Hannover. Ministerial head and division head of the Hessian department for women's affairs. 1990–92 planning of the Schweizer Design Center in Langenthal. 1992–94 Director of the 'Forum' at the Kunst- und Ausstellungshalle of the Federal Republic of Germany in Bonn. Since 1995 professor for gender studies and design as well as qualitative design research at the Cologne International School of Design. First Chairwoman of the German Society for Design Theory and Research (DGTF). Research focus: gender-related design; sex – body, sexualised products; new approaches to empirical design research.

Luzie Bratner (b. 1969)

Art historian (Dr. phil.). Studied art history, classical archaeology and Italian language and literature in Mainz and Vienna. Wrote her thesis on German Funerary Sculpture of the 17th and 18th centuries. Since 2000 has worked at the Museum of Applied Art Cologne. Research focus: European Baroque and Rococo painting and sculpture.

Patricia Brattig (b. 1968)

Art historian (Dr. phil.). Studied art history, Romance languages and classical archaeology in Cologne and Paris. Doctorate in 1998 with a thesis on 'The Château of Vaux-le-Vicomte'. Since 1998 has worked at the Museum of Applied Art Cologne, since 2000 as head curator of fashion and textile as well as glass and ceramics departments. Research focus: French architecture and interior decoration of the 17th and 18th centuries; history of fashion; tapestries.

Karen Ellwanger (b. 1953)

Cultural historian (Professor Dr. phil.). Studied empirical cultural history, rhetoric and sociology in Tübingen and comparative textile studies in Dortmund. Doctorate in 1994 with a thesis on 'Clothing in the Process of Modernisation 1870–1930. Women, Fashion, Mobility'. Since 1982 has taught and researched at several universities (Tübingen, Osnabrück, Ulm, Göttingen, Dortmund, Solothurn) and the Hochschule der Künste in Berlin. Since 1994 Professor for the cultural history of European textiles at Carl von Ossietzky University in Oldenburg, since 2003 at the 'Art-Textile-Media' Institute. Dean of the collegiate and doctoral studies programme 'Cultural History and Gender Studies'. Research focus: clothing and body image in Modernism; vestimentary representation of the political; empirical lifestyle research.

Elke Gaugele (b. 1964)

Empirical cultural historian (Dr. phil.). Studied European ethnology, history and political science in Berlin, Tübingen and Vienna. A curator for several years, she took her doctorate in 1999 with a thesis on 'Clothing as the Medium of Gender Constructs'. Currently working on her post-doctoral thesis at the Institute for Art and Art Theory, Textiles Department, Cologne University. Fellowship at Goldsmiths College, London (2003/2004) and Maria-Goeppert-Mayer Visiting Professor for International Gender Research (2004). Research focus: gender constructs at the interface of body and clothing; fashion, consumerism and visual culture; field research and performative process.

Eva Gronbach (b. 1971)

Fashion designer. After finishing high school, served an apprenticeship as a ladies' bespoke tailor in Düsseldorf, in 1995 certificate (Gesellenbrief). 1995 to 2000 studied 'Style and Fashion Creation' for a diploma at the Institut supérieur des arts visuels La Cambre in Brussels. In 1997 on-the-job training with Stephen Jones in London. In 1998 Erasmus exchange student at the Institut français de la Mode in Paris (degree: 'European Master of Art'). In 1999 practical training with Yohji Yamamoto in Paris. Has worked for John Galliano and Hermès. Since 2000 self-employed fashion designer in Cologne.

Ingrid Heimann (b. 1934)

Art historian (Professor Dr. phil.). Studied art teaching at the Staatliche Hochschule für Bildende Künste Berlin and art history, mathematics and information science at Berlin Technical University. In 1963 inspector of teachers at state schools. In 1972 professor for the theory of design at the Hochschule der Künste Berlin. Research focus: clothing formalities.

Abbildungsverzeichnis

54 Chiffonkleid, Lichtenberg/Oberfranken, um 1933/37, aus dem Besitz von Blanche Marteau (gest. 1977), Ehefrau des französischen Geigers Henri Marteau (1874–1934), Seidenchiffon, Unterkleid fehlt, Schenkung Felicitas Rüben, Köln (2002), MAK Köln, Inv.Nr. P 990

55 Abendensemble, Deutschland, um 1936/38, Oberteil und Gürtel: Cloqué aus Seide, farbig bedruckt mit Lancierung aus versilbertem Kupferlahn, Rock: Crêpe-Satin aus schwarzer Seide, Nachlass Leonora Elisabeth Gräfin von Schlitz, genannt von Görtz und von Wrisberg, Frankfurt (1990), MAK Köln, Inv.Nr. P 1014

56 „Kleines Schwarzes", Deutschland (?), um 1945, leinwandbindiges Gewebe mit leichter Rippenstruktur aus schwarzer Seide oder regenerierter Cellulosefaser (?), Schenkung Barbara Broich, Bergisch Gladbach, MAK Köln, Inv.Nr. P 1020

57 Abendkleid, Salon Stuckenberger, München, um 1945/46, Taffetas moiré quadrillé aus regenerierter Cellulosefaser, Schenkung Henriette Zoellner, Köln (1993), MAK Köln, Inv.Nr. P 779

58 „Kleines Schwarzes", Wien oder Königsberg, um 1945/47, Oberteil: schwarze Maschinenspitze auf cremefarbener Gaze, Rock: schwarzes Kunstfaser-Kreppgewebe, Schenkung Ute E. Ruster, Troisdorf-Eschmar (1993), MAK Köln, Inv.Nr. P 761

59 Sommer-Ensemble mit Hut, Deutschland, um 1952, Everglaze: gelbes Baumwollgewebe, schwarz bedruckt und anschließend gaufriert, Hut: gelb gefärbtes und geflochtenes Stroh mit schwarzer Fransenborte aus Bast und Flechtborte aus Stroh als Halteriemen, Schenkung Erbengemeinschaft Lueg, Düsseldorf (2003), MAK Köln, Inv.Nr. P 1029

60 Glockenrock mit Bluse, Modehaus Horn, Berlin und Hamburg, um 1953/54, Rock: Piquée aus Baumwolle, rot-weiß gestreift, Baumwollborte, Bluse: Piquée aus Baumwolle, Baumwollborte, Baumwoll-Zackenlitze, Schenkung Heilwig Ahlers-von der Mehden, Bonn (1989 und 1993), MAK Köln, Inv.Nr. P 189

61 Etuikleid, Emanuel Ungaro, Paris, um 1965, orangefarbenes Kreppgewebe aus Wolle, Schenkung Dr. Ursula Diederichs-Helf, Düsseldorf (1994), MAK Köln, Inv.Nr. P 869

62 Cocktailkleid aus Metallplättchen, Paco Rabanne, Paris, um 1966/67, Aluminium, Leihgabe Dieter Pool, Köln

63 Cocktailkleid in Silber, Kupfer und Orangerot, Ponater Modelle, Preysing-Palais, München, um 1967/69, Jacquardgewebe aus Baumwolle und Chemiefaser mit Schußeinträgen aus Metallahn, Schenkung Margret Garde, Bergisch Gladbach (2002), MAK Köln, Inv.Nr. P 1030

64 Partykleid mit Op-Art-Muster, Boltze-Modell, Deutschland, um 1965/70, bedrucktes Baumwollgewebe, Schenkung Prof. Dr. Otto-Friedrich und Irmgard Timmermann, Köln (1991), MAK Köln, Inv.Nr. P 589

65 Hosenanzug, Deutschland, um 1970, bedruckte Kulierware aus texturiertem Garn (Banilon), Schenkung Edith Klussmann, Köln (2002), MAK Köln, Inv.Nr. P 1021

66 Cocktailensemble, Emilio Pucci, Florenz, Prêt-à-porter um 1974/75, Rock: bedruckter Baumwollsamt und Seide, Bluse: Köper aus bedruckter Seide, Schenkung Marianne Hilfrich, Köln (1989), MAK Köln, Inv.Nr. P 229

67 Ensemble aus Pullover, Rock und Schärpe, Yves Saint Laurent Rive Gauche, Paris, Prêt-à-porter Frühjahr/Sommer 1984, Pullover: doppelseitige Kulierware (Fil d'Écosse) aus Baumwolle, Rock und Schärpe: Gabardine aus bedruckter Baumwolle, Schenkung Hedwig Neven DuMont, Köln (2002), MAK Köln, Inv.Nr. P 1002

68 Ensemble aus Bluse, Rock und Schärpe, Deutschland, um 1980/81, royalblau/schwarz karierte Tussah-Seide, Schenkung Dr. Michael Schroedel, Nürnberg (2003), MAK Köln, Inv.Nr. P 1022

69 Korsettkleid mit konischen Brüsten, Jean Paul Gaultier, Paris, Prêt-à-porter Herbst/Winter 1984/85, Seidensamt, Provenienz: Archives Jean Paul Gaultier SA, Paris

70 Abendensemble, Thierry Mugler, Paris, Haute Couture 1985, weißer Crêpe sablé aus regenerierter Cellulosefaser (?), anonyme Schenkung (2002), MAK Köln, Inv.Nr. P 1006

71 „Kleines Schwarzes" (Cocktailkleid), Azzedine Alaïa, Paris, Prêt-à-porter um 1985/87, schwarzes Stretchgewebe aus Rayon und Elasthan, schwarze Maschenware, Sammlung Jeane Freifrau von Oppenheim, Köln (2003), MAK Köln, Inv.Nr. P 1012

72 Rotes Kleid, Moschino, Mailand, Prêt-à-porter um 1986/87, leinwandbindiges Gewebe aus Acetat und Viskose, in der Taille schwarze Kulierware mit Patentmuster aus Acetat oder Viskose, Schenkung Gabriele Kortmann, Köln (2002), MAK Köln, Inv.Nr. P 1019

73 Romeo Gigli, Mailand, Herbst/Winter 1989/90, wasserfallartiger Samtmantel aus Baumwolle, bestickt mit güldenem Garn und güldenen Metallblumen, Leihgabe Romeo Gigli, Mailand

74 Nadelstreifenkostüm mit Schößchenjacke und Binderock, Vivienne Westwood, London, Prêt-à-porter um 1993, Tuch aus Schurwolle, Futter aus Acetat, Metallknöpfe mit dem Symbol der Entwerferin (Reichsapfel

mit Saturnring), Schenkung Dr. Adele Schlombs, Köln (2002), MAK Köln, Inv.Nr. P 979

75 „Roboter" aus der Kollektion „Cirque d'Hiver", Thierry Mugler, Paris, Prêt-à-porter Herbst/Winter 1995/96, silberfarbenes Metall, Plexiglas, violetter Mantel aus Satin Duchesse, Leihgabe Thierry Mugler, Paris

76 Tagesensemble „Princesse Partabgarh", Christian Dior, Design: John Galliano, Paris, Haute Couture Herbst/Winter 1997/98, Nr. 19, geschweifter, langer Gehrock (Whipcord aus kaffeebrauner Wolle) mit hohem Reverskragen, engen Kimonoärmeln und Dior-Pattentaschen an den Hüften, vom Saum ausgehend mit Velours appliqué und Jet in floralen Girlanden bestickt, in schrägem Fadenverlauf zugeschnittener „Sirenen"-Rock aus schwarzem Crêpe, schwarze Guêpière, Maharadjah-Schmuck, Hut von Stephen Jones (London), Leihgabe Christian Dior Archives, Paris

77 Roter Mantel aus der Kollektion „Body meets Dress", Comme des Garçons, Rei Kawakubo, Paris, Prêt-à-porter Frühjahr/Sommer 1997, Nylon, Polyurethane, Füllung aus Gänsefedern, Leihgabe Thomas Grünfeld, Köln

78 Grau-weiß kariertes Kleid aus der Kollektion „Body meets Dress", Comme des Garçons, Rei Kawakubo, Paris, Prêt-à-porter Frühjahr/Sommer 1997, diverse Materialien, Leihgabe Katharina Evers, Köln

79 Stehende mit erhobenem Arm, Ludwig Gabriel Schrieber, Berlin, 1955. Aus: Neuer Berliner Kunstverein, Ausst.Kat. Berlin 1975

80–95 Archiv Heimann, Berlin

96 Kleid aus der Kollektion „Welcome Little Stranger", UFO-Thema, Walter van Beirendonck, Antwerpen, Prêt-à-porter Frühjahr/Sommer 1997, nichtgewebte, bedruckte Textilie (non tissé), Perücke aus synthetischem Haar, Blumen und Bienen, Leihgabe Walter van Beirendonck, Antwerpen

97 Chiffonkleid, Dries van Noten, Antwerpen, Prêt-à-porter Frühjahr/Sommer 1998, Crêpe de Chine aus bedruckter Seide, anonyme Schenkung (2002), MAK Köln, Inv.Nr. P 1004

98 Tschador-Sequenz, Hussein Chalayan, London, Frühjahr/Sommer 1998, Viskose, Leihgabe Hussein Chalayan, London

99 Abendkleid mit Schlaufenblende, Christian Dior, Paris, Prêt-à-porter um 1999, Crêpe-Satin aus Acetat und Viskose, Schenkung Heinrich Becker, Köln (2002), MAK Köln, Inv.Nr. P 1007

100 A.F. Vandevorst, Antwerpen, Frühjahr/Sommer 2001, Leder-Bustier „Alarm", Baumwoll-Faltenrock „Sonic", Lederstiefel, Leihgabe A.F. Vandevorst, Antwerpen

101 Kollektion „Sein und Schein", Elternhaus® Maegde u. Knechte®, Hamburg, 2001, Hermès-Jacke „Pferde", Ripp-Shirt „Goethe Gucci", Schuhe „Goethe – Hegel – Kant / Nike", Tasche „Jil Sander – Elbe Obst", Leihgabe Elternhaus® Maegde u. Knechte® aus Privatbesitz, Hamburg

102 Kollektion „Liebeserklärung an Deutschland", Eva Gronbach, Köln, 2002, Fahnenpullover in schwarzem, rotem, und gelbem Niki aus Baumwolle, schwarzer Rock aus Baumwolle, Ledertasche in Schwarz, Rot und Gelb, Birkenstock-Schuhe, Leihgabe Eva Gronbach, Köln

103 Martin Margiela, Paris, Herbst/Winter 2001/02, Nr. 8, Jackenkleid, Tabi-Lederstiefel, am Knöchel geschlitzt, Leihgabe Maison Martin Margiela, Paris

104 Martin Margiela, Paris, Herbst/Winter 2001/02, Nr. 23, übergroße Wolljacke, gepreßte Vintage-Kleider, Schal aus Vintage-Nerzmantelteilen, Tabi-Overknees aus Leder, Leihgabe Maison Martin Margiela, Paris

105 Rosa Kleid aus der Kollektion „Afrika", Bernhard Willhelm, Antwerpen, Prêt-à-porter Herbst/Winter 2001/02, Baumwolle, Leihgabe Heimat, Andreas Hoyer und Andy Scherpereel, Köln

106 Kleid aus der Kollektion „The Gipsy in me ...", Darja Richter, Paris, Prêt-à-porter Herbst/Winter 2002/03, Baby-Merino, gearbeitet auf Tüll mit Chantilly-Spitze und Glasperlen, Leihgabe Darja Richter, Paris

107 Milano Show Collection, Strenesse Gabriele Strehle, Nördlingen, Herbst/Winter 2002/03, Nr. 31, marineblaue Seidenjacke, mit Drachenmotiv bestickt, schwarzes Wollkleid, Leihgabe Strenesse Gabriele Strehle, Nördlingen

108 Milano Show Collection, Strenesse Gabriele Strehle, Nördlingen, Herbst/Winter 2002/03, Nr. 36, marineblaues Seidenkleid, mit Drachenmotiv bestickt, schwarze Wollhose, Leihgabe Strenesse Gabriele Strehle, Nördlingen

109–114 Lilith & Burkhard im Atelier, Köln, Juli 2003

115 CHANEL, Design: Karl Lagerfeld, Paris, Haute Couture Frühjahr/Sommer 2003, Nr. 22, weißer Tweed-Spenzer mit schwarzem Samtkragen und Manschetten, schwarzer Tüllrock, Leihgabe CHANEL, Paris

116 Christian Dior, Design: John Galliano, Paris, Haute Couture Frühjahr/Sommer 2003, Nr. 23, besticktes, gestreiftes Seidentaftkleid mit Saum aus Organzavolants, mehrlagiger Chiffon-Bolero in Pink, Leihgabe Christian Dior Archives, Paris

117–118 „Ultramarine", Jean Paul Gaultier, Paris, Haute Couture Frühling/Sommer 2003, Nr. 41, Marinepullover „Surprise" aus Organza, mit blauen Perlmuttknöpfen gestreift, langer, in Rot und Elfenbein gestreifter Tüllrock aus Seide, Provenienz: Archives Jean Paul Gaultier SA, Paris

119 Stephan Schneider, Antwerpen, Frühjahr/Sommer 2003, Blouson und Rock aus selbstentworfenem Jacquard-Jersey mit typographischem Muster, bestickte, ärmellose und gestreifte Baumwollbluse, Legging aus Baumwolljersey und Spitze, gefältete Lederschuhe, Leihgabe Stephan Schneider, Antwerpen
120 Abendjogginganzug, Bernhard Willhelm, Antwerpen, Prêt-à-porter Frühjahr/Sommer 2003, Seide und Baumwolle, Leihgabe Heimat, Andreas Hoyer und Andy Scherpereel, Köln
121 Bikini „Genoveva", Halstuch „Benedetta", Rock „Ludovica", goyagoya, Darmstadt, Design: Elena Zenero Hock, Frühling/Sommer 2003, Polyamid, Polyester und Seide, Leihgabe goyagoya, Darmstadt
122 Milano Show Collection, Strenesse Gabriele Strehle, Nördlingen, Herbst/Winter 2003/04, Nr. 30, schwarzes Minikleid aus Kaschmir, Leihgabe Strenesse Gabriele Strehle, Nördlingen
123 Hermès, Paris, Prêt-à-porter Herbst/Winter 2003/04, Nr. 18, Blouson mit weiten Ärmeln aus ockerfarbener Kaschmirwolle in Double-face-Verarbeitung, nahtloser Kaschmir-Pullover mit rundem Halsausschnitt und Fledermausärmeln, Serge-Hose aus naturfarbenem Kamelhaar, Leihgabe Hermès, Paris
124 Kollektion „Astral Amazon", Romeo Gigli, Mailand, Herbst/Winter 2003/04, Nr. 37, schulterfreies Top mit Flügelärmeln aus Wolle, bestickt mit silberfarbenem Garn, asymmetrischer, plissierter Rock aus Wolle, Metallahn und Seide, Leihgabe Romeo Gigli, Mailand
125 Abendensemble „Soir", Liz Weinmann, Köln, Prêt-à-porter Herbst/Winter 2003/04, Kleid: schwarze Maschenware aus Viskose, Jacke: Taffetas glacé mit unregelmäßigem Plissee aus Polyamid, Schenkung Liz Weinmann, Köln (2003), MAK Köln, Inv.Nr. P 1028
126 Kollektion Bless N°19 uncool, Bless, Paris/Berlin, Herbst/Winter 2003/04, Poncho aus Wolle, bedrucktes Sweatshirt aus Baumwolle, grauer Overall aus Wolle, grauer Ledergürtel, Leihgabe Bless, Paris/Berlin
127 Ja!-Outfit, Ja!-Jungs, Offenbach, Sommer 2003, langärmeliges Baumwollhemd, Baumwollrock mit selbstklebender Velourfolie, Lederschuhe, Leihgabe Ja!-Jungs, Offenbach
128 Lutz, Paris, Herbst/Winter 2003/04, Jacke mit roten Fransen aus Wolle und Baumwolle, Tankkleid aus Baumwolle und Kuhfell-Clogs, Leihgabe Lutz, Paris
129–131 Diana Gärtner in der Deutschen Botschaft in Paris, Kollektion „Déclaration d'amour à l'Allemagne", Eva Gronbach, Köln, 2000, Fotoshooting gesponsort von Wolfgang van Moers
132–134 Aline, Xenia und Hodan im Bonner Kanzleramt, Kabinettsaal, Kollektion „Liebeserklärung an Deutschland", Eva Gronbach, Köln, 2002
135 „Bird" aus der Kollektion „South", Stephen Jones, London, Frühjahr/Sommer 2003, diverse Materialien, Leihgabe Stephen Jones, London
136 „Snowstrobe" aus der Kollektion „South", Stephen Jones, London, Frühjahr/Sommer 2003, diverse Materialien, Leihgabe Stephen Jones, London
137 „Myth" aus der Kollektion „South", Stephen Jones, London, Frühjahr/Sommer 2003, diverse Materialien, Leihgabe Stephen Jones, London
138 „Striking" aus der Kollektion „South", Stephen Jones, London, Frühjahr/Sommer 2003, diverse Materialien, Leihgabe Stephen Jones, London
139 „Emperor" aus der Kollektion „South", Stephen Jones, London, Frühjahr/Sommer 2003, diverse Materialien, Leihgabe Stephen Jones, London

Illustrations

1–3 Robe à la française, Germany (?), ca. 1780, Gros de Tours liseré, piped silk brocade, gift of Robert Peill, Cologne (1901), Museum of Applied Art Cologne (= MAK Köln), inv.no. D 1002
4–5 Chemise dress, Germany (?), ca. 1810, cotton muslin with cotton embroidery, MAK Köln, Courtesy Kölnisches Stadtmuseum, inv.no. T 634
6 François Gérard, Juliette Récamier, 1800/02, oil on canvas, Paris, Musée Carnavalet, inv.no. P 1581
7 Christian Gottlieb Schick, Wilhelmine von Cotta, 1802, oil on canvas, Staatsgalerie Stuttgart, inv.no. GVL 87
8 'A faithful likeness of Madame Tallien in Paris, as she recently appeared at the grand ball in the Opera. [...] Her whole arm – the most beautiful to be seen – is bare. [...] Her dress is caught up to the knee on the left side [...] so that it exposes the whole leg to the lustful eye.', copperplate engraving from the Journal für Fabrik, Manufaktur, Handlung und Mode, Leipzig 1797, Vol. 12 (June 1797), pl. IV, p. 473f.
9 Sample coupons 'No. 1 is an English half silk fabric which is often worn with gentlemen's waistcoats and is also very often worn with ladies' dresses because it is so lightweight. It is 5/4 ells wide. It costs 2 Reichstaler, 2 to 6 groschen the ell. No. 2. A brocaded muslin from the Plaue Factory intended for ladies' dresses. Among the large stars in the stripe even smaller flowers are woven in which could not be made discernible in this sample. It is 5/4 ells wide. It is sold for 22 groschen to 1 Reichs taler the ell.' Samples table from the Journal für Fabrik, Manufaktur, Handlung und Mode, Leipzig, Vol. 13 (July 1797), p. 76f.
10 'Two ladies dressed in the newest French fashion taking friendly leave of one another.', copperplate engraving from the Journal für Fabrik, Manufaktur, Handlung und Mode, Leipzig 1797, Vol. 13 (August 1797), pl. IV, p. 155
11 'The newest fashions in costume.' On no. 1: 'The head-dress of the lady above no. 1 consists in a white muslin band, tied in a bow at the front. [...] The chemise with half-length sleeves is also muslin. [...] The scarf across the breast of finest linen. [...] The shoes are of white Coralline point (needlepoint), faced on the sides with black Morocco leather. Since this costume is intended for dancing, silver shoe tips would be unnecessary.', copperplate engraving from the Journal für Fabrik, Manufaktur, Handlung und Mode, Leipzig 1798, Vol. 14 (April 1798), pl. IV, p. 322f.
12 Merveilleuse, late 18th century. Etching by Auguste Étienne Guillaumot from Costumes du Directoire Tirés des Merveilleuses, Paris 1875, pl. 25
13 'A lady in the newest fashion in costume. [...] The lady's dress follows the most current fashion in openwork brocaded muslin.', copperplate engraving from the Journal für Fabrik, Manufaktur, Handlung und Mode, Leipzig 1800, Vol. 18 (May 1800), pl. III, p. 435
14 Chemise dress (back), Germany (?), ca. 1819, toile with cotton flat point and hollie-work embroidery, silk lace trim, MAK Köln, Courtesy Kölnisches Stadtmuseum, inv.no. T 440
15 Summer dress, Germany (?), ca. 1829, cotton muslin with cotton flat point embroidery and knotted lace, MAK Köln, Courtesy Kölnisches Stadtmuseum, inv.no. T 8
16 Afternoon dress with ‚leg of mutton' sleeves, Germany (?), ca. 1830/31, mouse grey to silvery silk, linen-weft (toile) with drawn-work patterns formed by whipped-over warp, purchased in 1985, MAK Köln, inv.no. P 21
17 Afternoon dress with ‚pagoda' sleeves, Germany, Cologne (?), ca. 1848/50, drawn-work silk toile, trimmed with bands of black silk velvet, MAK Köln, Courtesy Kölnisches Stadtmuseum, inv.no. T 18
18 Parisian costumes, 1819, copperplate engraving from the Journal des Dames et des Modes, No. 27, fashion plate 27
19 Carl Begas, The Begas Family, 1821, oil on canvas, Cologne, Wallraf-Richartz Museum / Fondation Corboud, inv.no. 1556
20 Parisian costumes, 1829, copperplate engraving from the Journal des Dames et des Modes, No. 45, fashion plate 45
21 Parisian costumes, 1830, copperplate engraving from the Journal des Dames et des Modes, No. 17, fashion plate 17
22 German and French costumes, 1831, copperplate engraving from the Journal des Dames et des Modes, No. 21, fashion plate 21
23 Simon Meister, The Werbrun Family, 1834, oil on canvas, Cologne, Wallraf-Richartz Museum / Fondation Corboud, inv.no. 1113
24 Copper fashion plate from the Allgemeine Modenzeitung, 1841, no. 31
25 Copper fashion plate from the Allgemeine Modenzeitung, 1843, no. 24
26 Afternoon dress (crinoline), Germany or Great Britain (?), ca. 1866, red/green/blue/black tartan taffeta, edges emphasised with green satin piping, trimmed with a green gimp border and tassels, purchased in 1987, MAK Köln, Courtesy Overstolzengesellschaft, inv.no. Ov 181

27 Afternoon dress, Great Britain (?), ca. 1869/70, taffeta, purple and yellow stripes, trimmed with velvet ribbon and fringe, purchased in 1985, MAK Köln, inv.no. P 23

28 Afternoon dress, ca. 1872/74, brown gros de Tours silk, purchased in 1985, MAK Köln, inv.no. P 27

29 Afternoon dress, Miss Williams, Great Britain, 51 Portland St., Fareham, ca. 1881/82, taffeta with linen thread, pattern effect achieved by different coloured threads in warp and weft, light grey ground with a fine dark grey check, contrasting dark grey unpatterned taffeta on the cuffs, centre front and hemline, purchased in 1985, MAK Köln, inv.no. P 30

30 Day dress with 'cul de Paris' bustle, ca. 1884/86, printed beige cotton, edged with lace, purchased in 1985, MAK Köln, inv.no. P 29

31 Afternoon dress, Schollmeyer & Böhme, purveyors to the court, Magdeburg, ca. 1894/95, red silk satin dress trimmed in green voile, on the sleeves brocaded silk chambray, patterns formed by differences both in dyeing between weft and warp and in weave, gift of Gisela Suckert-Martini, Cologne (2002), MAK Köln, inv.no. P 993

32 Henry van de Velde, velvet dress in a fashionable colour with light brown and dark grey appliqués and crewel embroidery. From: Mohrbutter 1904, p. 11

33 'On the harm to adipose distribution.' From: Schultze-Naumburg 1910, p. 88f.

34 Cover of the book 'Das Kleid der Frau' ['The Lady's Dress'] by Alfred Mohrbutter. Darmstadt, Leipzig 1904

35 The Venus de Milo. From: Schultze-Naumburg 1910, p. 17

36 Anatomical analysis. From: Schultze-Naumburg 1910, p. 18f.

37 Anna Muthesius, indoor dress, greyish lavender fabric with dull green appliqués. From: Mohrbutter 1904, p. 7

38 Reform dress (wedding dress), Cologne, 1898, lined dress of cream silk satin, outer garment of cream silk crêpe georgette, silk and cotton netting, tulle trimmed with braiding, gift of Lotte Scheibler, Cologne (1958), MAK Köln, Courtesy Kölnisches Stadtmuseum, inv.no. T 356

39 Reform dress (summer dress), Germany (?), ca. 1909, cotton batiste with needlepoint lace (buttonhole and flat embroidery), bobbin lace at the collar, trimming the sleeves and yoke, purchased in 1985, MAK Köln, inv.no. P 8

40 Evening dress, Great Britain (?), ca. 1903/07, satin embroidered with black sequins and faceted glass beads, sleeve fabric woven in checks, purchased in 1985, MAK Köln, inv.no. P 38

41 Afternoon dress, Berlin, 1926/27, red silk crêpe de Chine, tulle lace (machine-made) of silk or artificial silk, gift of Hedy Brepohl, Cologne (1990), MAK Köln, inv.no. P 314

42 Evening dress, attributed to Callot Sœurs, Paris, ca. 1927/29, sateen embroidered with wax and glass beads as well as glass stones, greenish yellow silk velvet, green silk lining, purchased in 1994, MAK Köln, inv.no. P 814

43 Chiffon dress, Germany, ca. 1928/30, printed silk chiffon, gift of Ellen Thienhaus, Cologne (2002), MAK Köln, inv.no. P 959

44 Ensemble, sweater and skirt, illustration from *Vogue*, 1928. From: Thiel 1990, p. 398

45 Costume with blouse, illustration from *Vogue*, 1928. From: Thiel 1990, p. 398

46 Coat with fur stole worn over skirt and sweater, illustration from *Vogue*, 1928. From: Thiel 1990, p. 398

47 'Au loup!' Dress in 'corn flowers' in a 'floral garland' by Rodier', colour lithograph from the *Gazette du Bon Ton*, no. 4, 1921, pl. 26, MAK Köln, Departement of Prints and Drawings, acquisition no. 1973/33

48 Dress designs by Alexandra Exter, illustration from *Atelier*, 1923. From: Thiel 1990, p. 392

49 Amateur snapshot, Berlin, 1926

50 Fashion drawing by Hete Behrens, Cologne, ca. 1931, pen and pencil with wash, gift of Georg Perrin, Cologne (2003), MAK Köln, Departement of Prints and Drawings

51 Fashion plate, 'Original Models', no. 397, Atelier Bachwitz, ca. 1925, colour lithograph, purchased in 1986, MAK Köln, Departement of Prints and Drawings, inv.no. C 555c

52 Fashion drawing by Hete Behrens, Cologne, ca. 1930/31, pencil drawing washed with watercolour, gift of Georg Perrin, Cologne (2003), MAK Köln, Departement of Prints and Drawings

53 Black jumper with slacks, pleated at the waist in the Marlene Dietrich look, Germany, 1930s/'40s, jumper: Anne Marie Stuttgart, black stockinet jersey, wool, border of smooth gold (crocheted), slacks: light grey wool serge, gift of Ellen Thienhaus, Cologne (2002), MAK Köln, inv.nos. P 962 and P 964

54 Chiffon dress, Lichtenberg, Upper Franconia, ca. 1933/37, from the estate of Blanche Marteau (d. 1977), wife of the French violinist Henri Marteau (1974–1934), silk chiffon, lining missing, gift of Felicitas Rüben, Cologne (2002), MAK Köln, inv.no. P 990

55 Evening ensemble, Germany, ca. 1936/38, bodice and belt: silk cloqué, printed in colour, with silvered copper foil designs going through the thickness

of the material, skirt: black satin crêpe, from the estate of Leonora Elisabeth, Countess von Schlitz, genannt Görtz und von Wrisberg, Frankfurt (1990), MAK Köln, inv.no. P 1014

56 'Little Black Dress', Germany (?), ca. 1945, twill fabric, slightly ribbed texture of black silk or reclaimed cellulose fibre (?), gift of Barbara Broich, Bergisch Gladbach, MAK Köln, inv.no. P 1020

57 Evening dress, Salon Stuckenberger, Munich, ca. 1945/46, chequered moiré taffeta of reclaimed cellulose fibre, gift of Henriette Zoellner, Cologne (1993), MAK Köln, inv.no. P 779

58 'Little Black Dress', Vienna or Königsberg, ca. 1945/47, bodice: black machine-made lace over cream gauze, both of reclamed cellulose fibre, skirt: black synthetic crape, gift of Ute E. Ruster, Troisdorf-Eschmar (1993), MAK Köln, inv.no. P 761

59 Summer ensemble with hat, Germany, ca. 1952, Everglaze: yellow cotton fabric, black print, crimped, hat: yellow dyed woven straw with black fringed raffia band and woven straw band to tie under the chin, gift joint heirs Lueg, Düsseldorf (2003), MAK Köln, inv.no. P 1029

60 Flared skirt with blouse, Modehaus Horn, Berlin and Hamburg, ca. 1953/54, skirt: cotton piqué, red and white stripes, cotton edging, blouse: cotton piqué, cotton edging, cotton scalloping, gift of Heilwig Ahlers-von der Mehden, Bonn (1989 and 1993), MAK Köln, inv.no. P 189

61 Sheath gown, Emanuel Ungaro, Paris, ca. 1965, orange wool crape, gift of Dr. Ursula Diederichs-Helf, Düsseldorf (1994), MAK Köln, inv.no. P 869

62 Cocktail dress of metal disks, Paco Rabanne, Paris, ca. 1966/67, aluminium, Courtesy Dieter Pool, Cologne

63 Cocktail dress in silver, copper and reddish orange, Ponater Modelle, Preysing-Palais, Munich, ca. 1967/69, jacquard weave of cotton and synthetic fibre shot with metal foil, gift of Margret Garde, Bergisch Gladbach (2002), MAK Köln, inv.no. P 1030

64 Party dress with Op Art pattern, Boltze-Modell, Germany, ca. 1965/70, cotton print, gift of Professor Dr. Otto-Friedrich and Irmgard Timmermann, Cologne (1991), MAK Köln, inv.no. P 589

65 Trouser suit, Germany, ca. 1970, printed stockinet jersey, textured yarn (Banilon), gift of Edith Klussmann, Cologne (2002), MAK Köln, inv.no. P 1021

66 Cocktail ensemble, Emilio Pucci, Florence, ready-to-wear, ca. 1974/75, skirt: printed cotton velvet and silk, blouse: printed silk twill, gift of Marianne Hilfrich, Cologne (1989), MAK Köln, inv.no. P 229

67 Ensemble, pullover, skirt and scarf, Yves Saint Laurent Rive Gauche, Paris, ready-to-wear spring/summer 1984, pullover: reversible cotton stockinet jersey (fil d'Écosse), skirt and scarf: printed cotton gabardine, gift of Hedwig Neven DuMont, Cologne (2002), MAK Köln, inv.no. P 1002

68 Ensemble, blouse, skirt and scarf, Germany, ca. 1980/81, royal blue/black checked tussore silk, gift of Dr. Michael Schroedel, Nürnberg (2003), MAK Köln, inv.no. P 1022

69 Corset dress with conical breast cups, Jean Paul Gaultier, Paris, ready-to-wear fall/winter 1984/85, silk velvet, provenance: Archives Jean Paul Gaultier SA, Paris

70 Evening ensemble, Thierry Mugler, Paris, haute couture 1985, white crêpe sablé of reclaimed cellulose fibre (?), anonymous gift (2002), MAK Köln, inv.no. P 1006

71 'Little Black Dress' (cocktail dress), Azzedine Alaïa, Paris, ready-to-wear ca. 1985/87, black stretch fabric of Rayon and Elasthan, black knitwear, Jeane Freifrau von Oppenheim Collection, Cologne (2003), MAK Köln, inv.no. P 1012

72 Red dress, Moschino, Milan, ready-to-wear ca. 1986/87, acetate and viscose fabric, at the waist black stockinet jersey with patent pattern of acetate or viscose, gift of Gabriele Kortmann, Cologne (2002), MAK Köln, inv.no. P 1019

73 Romeo Gigli, Milan, fall/winter 1989/90, waterfall cotton velvet cloak, embroidered with gold thread and gold metal flowers, Courtesy Romeo Gigli, Milan

74 Pin-stripe costume, jacket with tails, skirt, Vivienne Westwood, London, ready-to-wear ca. 1993, pure wool cloth, acetate lining, metal buttons with the designer's logo (imperial orb with rings of Saturn), gift of Dr. Adele Schlombs, Cologne (2002), MAK Köln, inv.no. P 979

75 'Robot' from the 'Cirque d'Hiver' collection, Thierry Mugler, Paris, ready-to-wear fall/winter 1995/96, silver-coloured metal, perspex, purple coat in Duchesse satin, Courtesy Thierry Mugler, Paris

76 Day ensemble 'Princesse Partabgarh', Christian Dior, Design: John Galliano, Paris, haute couture fall/winter 1997/98, no. 19, long shapely coffee wool whipcord frock-coat, plunging tailored collar, kimono glove sleeves, *Dior* flap pockets at the hips, embroidered with velvet appliqué and floral jet garlands from the hem upwards, *mermaid-line*-bias-cut black crêpe skirt, black waist-cincher, Maharaja jewellery, hat by Stephen Jones (London), Courtesy Christian Dior Archives, Paris

77 Red coat from the 'Body meets Dress' collection, Comme des Garçons, Rei Kawakubo, Paris, ready-to-wear spring/summer 1997, nylon, polyurethane, goose down filling, Courtesy Thomas Grünfeld, Cologne

78 Grey and white checked dress from the 'Body meets Dress' collection, Comme des Garçons, Rei Kawakubo, Paris, ready-to-wear spring/summer 1997, mixed media, Courtesy Katharina Evers, Cologne

79 Woman standing, her arm raised, by Ludwig Gabriel Schrieber, Berlin, 1955. From: Neuer Berliner Kunstverein [New Berlin Art Association], exhib. cat. Berlin 1975

80–95 Heimann Archives, Berlin

96 Dress from the 'Welcome little Stranger' collection, UFO-theme, Walter van Beirendonck, Antwerp, ready-to-wear spring/summer 1997, printed non-woven fabric, wig of synthetic hair, flowers and bees, Courtesy Walter van Beirendonck, Antwerp

97 Chiffon dress, Dries van Noten, Antwerp, ready-to-wear spring/summer 1998, printed crêpe de Chine, anonymous gift (2002), MAK Köln, inv.no. P 1004

98 Chador Sequence, Hussein Chalayan, London, spring/summer 1998, viscose, Courtesy Hussein Chalayan, London

99 Evening dress, Christian Dior, Paris, ready-to-wear, ca. 1999, acetate and viscose crape, gift of Heinrich Becker, Cologne (2002), MAK Köln, inv.no. P 1007

100 A.F. Vandevorst, Antwerp, spring/summer 2001, leather bustier 'Alarm', cotton pleated skirt 'Sonic', leather boots, Courtesy A.F. Vandevorst, Antwerp

101 'Being and Seeming' collection, Elternhaus® Maegde u. Knechte®, Hamburg, 2001, Hermès jacket 'Horses', ribbed shirt 'Goethe Gucci', shoes 'Goethe – Hegel – Kant / Nike'; bag 'Jil Sander – Elbe Obst', Courtesy Elternhaus® Maegde u. Knechte® and private collection, Hamburg

102 'A Declaration of Love to Germany' collection, Eva Gronbach, Cologne, 2002, flag pullover in black, red and yellow, cotton velour, black cotton skirt, leather bag in black, red and yellow, Birkenstock shoes, Courtesy Eva Gronbach, Cologne

103 Martin Margiela, Paris, fall/winter 2001/02, no. 18, artisanal jacket with its detached lining drops, transforming it into a dress, Tabi boots cut to the ankle, Courtesy Maison Martin Margiela, Paris

104 Martin Margiela, Paris, fall/winter 2001/02, no. 23, oversized jacket in wool, compressed vintage dresses, segments of vintage mink coats as scarf, thigh Tabi boots in leather, Courtesy Maison Martin Margiela, Paris

105 Pink dress from the 'Afrika' collection, Bernhard Willhelm, Antwerp, ready-to-wear fall/winter 2001/02, cotton, Courtesy Heimat, Andreas Hoyer and Andy Scherpereel, Cologne

106 Dress from the 'The Gipsy in me ...' collection, Darja Richter, Paris, ready-to-wear fall/winter 2002/03, baby merino worked on tulle with Chantilly lace and glass beads, Courtesy Darja Richter, Paris

107 Milano Show Collection, Strenesse Gabriele Strehle, Nördlingen, fall/winter 2002/03, no. 31, navy blue silk jacket embroidered with dragon motif, black wool dress, Courtesy Strenesse Gabriele Strehle, Nördlingen

108 Milano Show Collection, Strenesse Gabriele Strehle, Nördlingen, fall/winter 2002/03, Nr. 36, navy blue silk dress embroidered with dragon motif, black wool trousers, Courtesy Strenesse Gabriele Strehle, Nördlingen

109–114 Lilith & Burkhard in the MAK Köln, July 2003

115 CHANEL, design: Karl Lagerfeld, Paris, haute couture spring/summer 2003, no. 22, white tweed spencer with black velvet collar and cuffs, black tulle skirt, Courtesy CHANEL, Paris

116 Christian Dior, design: John Galliano, Paris, haute couture spring/summer 2003, no. 23, striped embroidered taffeta dress, hemmed with organza flounces, pink layered chiffon bolero, Courtesy Christian Dior Archives, Paris

117–118 'Ultramarine', Jean Paul Gaultier, Paris, haute couture spring/summer 2003, no. 41, organza navy pullover 'Surprise', long red and ivory striped tulle skirt with blue mother-of-pearl buttons, provenance: Archives Jean Paul Gaultier SA, Paris

119 Stephan Schneider, Antwerp, spring/summer 2003, windcheater jacket and skirt of Jacquard jersey with typographic pattern, embroidered striped cotton blouse without sleeves, leggings of cotton jersey and lace, pleated leather shoes, Courtesy Stephan Schneider, Antwerp

120 Evening jogging suit, Bernhard Willhelm, Antwerp, ready-to-wear spring/summer 2003, silk and cotton, Courtesy Heimat, Andreas Hoyer and Andy Scherpereel, Cologne

121 Bikini 'Genoveva', neck scarf 'Benedetta', skirt 'Ludovica', goyagoya, Darmstadt, design: Elena Zenero Hock, spring/summer 2003, polyamide, polyester and silk, Courtesy goyagoya, Darmstadt

122 Milano Show Collection, Strenesse Gabriele Strehle, Nördlingen, fall/winter 2003/04, no. 30, black cashmere mini dress, Courtesy Strenesse Gabriele Strehle, Nördlingen

123 Hermès, Paris, ready-to-wear fall/winter 2003/04, no. 18, windcheater jacket with wide sleeves of ochre double-face cashmere, seamless cashmere pullover with round neck and batwing sleeves, natural camel serge trousers, Courtesy Hermès, Paris

124 'Astral Amazon' collection, Romeo Gigli, Milan, fall/winter 2003/04, no. 37, off the shoulders wool top with wing sleeves, embroidered with silver thread, a-symmetrical pleated skirt in wool, metal and silk, Courtesy Romeo Gigli, Milan

125 Evening ensemble 'Soir', Liz Weinmann, Cologne, ready-to-wear fall/winter 2003/04, dress: black viscose net, jacket: glacé taffeta with irregular polyamide pleats, gift of Liz Weinmann, Cologne (2003), MAK Köln, inv.no. P 1028

126 Bless N° 19 uncool, Bless, Paris/Berlin, fall/winter 2003/04, wool poncho, printed cotton sweatshirt, grey wool overall, grey leather belt, Courtesy Bless, Paris/Berlin

127 Ja!-Outfit, Ja!-Jungs, Offenbach, summer 2003, cotton long-sleeved shirt, cotton skirt with self-sealing velour foil, leather shoes, Courtesy Ja!-Jungs, Offenbach

128 Lutz, Paris, fall/winter 2003/04, jacket with red fringes, tank dress, wool and cotton, clogs with cow hair, Courtesy Lutz, Paris

129–131 Diana Gärtner at the German Embassy in Paris, 'Declaration of Love to Germany' collection, Eva Gronbach, Cologne, 2000, photo session sponsored by Wolfgang van Moers

132–134 Aline, Xenia and Hodan at the Bonn Chancellery, Cabinet Chamber, 'Declaration of Love to Germany', Eva Gronbach, Cologne, 2002

135 'Bird' from the 'South' collection, Stephen Jones, London, spring/summer 2003, mexid media, Courtesy Stephen Jones, London

136 'Snowstrobe' from the 'South' collection, Stephen Jones, London, spring/summer 2003, mexid media, Courtesy Stephen Jones, London

137 'Myth' from the 'South' collection, Stephen Jones, London, spring/summer 2003, mixed media, Courtesy Stephen Jones, London

138 'Striking' from the 'South' collection, Stephen Jones, London, spring/summer 2003, mixed media, Courtesy Stephen Jones, London

139 'Emperor' from the 'South' collection, Stephen Jones, London, spring/summer 2003, mixed media, Courtesy Stephen Jones, London

Weiterführende Literatur / Further Reading

Addressing the Century. 100 Years of Art & Fashion. Ausst.-Kat. Hayward Gallery, London und Kunstmuseum Wolfsburg 1998/99. London 1998
Antoni-Komar, Irene (Hrsg.): Moderne Körperlichkeit. Körper als Orte ästhetischer Erfahrung. Stuttgart, Bremen 2001 = Mode und Ästhetik. Schriftenreihe des Instituts für Designforschung Bremen, Bd. I
Anziehungskräfte. Variété de la Mode. 1786–1986. Ausst.-Kat. Münchner Stadtmuseum. München 1986
Arnold, Rebecca: Fashion, Desire and Anxiety. Image and Morality in the 20th Century. London, New York 2001
Ashelford, Jane: The Art of Dress. Clothes and Society 1500–1914. London 1996
Barthes, Roland: Die Sprache der Mode. Frankfurt am Main 1985 = edition suhrkamp 1318, Neue Folge Band 318
Beirendonck, Walter van und Luc **Derycke** (Hrsg.): Mode 2001 Landed–Geland–Atterri. Ausst.-Kat. Merz, Antwerpen Open und Flanders Fashion Institute. 2 Bde. Antwerpen 2001
Bernsmeier, Uta: Im Gewand der Zeit. Mode der Jahrhundertwenden 1800 – 1900 – 2000. Ausst.-Kat. Bremer Landesmuseum für Kunst und Kulturgeschichte Focke-Museum. Bremen 2000 = Veröffentlichungen des Bremer Landesmuseums für Kunst und Kulturgeschichte Focke-Museum, Nummer 104
Black, J. Anderson und Madge **Garland**: A History of Fashion. London 1975
Boehn, Max von: Die Mode. Eine Kulturgeschichte vom Barock bis zum Jugendstil. Bearbeitet von Ingrid Loschek. München 1986
Bönsch, Annemarie: Formengeschichte europäischer Kleidung. Hrsg. von Gabriela Krist. Wien, Köln, Weimar 2001 = Konservierungswissenschaft, Restaurierung, Technologie, Bd. I
Bovenschen, Silvia (Hrsg.): Die Listen der Mode. Frankfurt am Main 1986 = edition suhrkamp 1338, Neue Folge Band 338
Braun-Ronsdorf, Margarete: Modische Eleganz. Europäische Kostümgeschichte von 1789 bis 1929. München 1963
Brock, Bazon und Matthias **Eberle**: Mode – das inszenierte Leben. Kleidung und Wohnung als Lernenvironment. Ausst.-Kat. Internationales Design Zentrum e.V. Berlin. Berlin o.J. = Paperback IDZ 4
Cunnington, Philis und C. **Willet**: The History of Underclothes. New York 1992
Deslandres, Yvonne und Florence **Müller**: Histoire de la Mode au XXe siècle. Paris 1986
Evans, Caroline und Minna **Thornton**: Women & Fashion. A New Look. London 1989
Ewing, Elizabeth: History of Twentieth Century Fashion. London 1986[3]
Fashion. Die Sammlung des Kyoto Costume Institute. Eine Modegeschichte vom 18. Jahrhundert bis 20. Jahrhundert. Bestandskatalog. Köln 2002
Fehlig, Ursula: Kostümkunde. Mode im Wandel der Zeiten. Leipzig 1980[3]
Femmes fin de siècle. 1885–1895. Ausst.-Kat. Musée de la Mode et du Costume Palais Galliera. Paris 1990
Haye, Amy de la und Elizabeth **Wilson** (Hrsg.): Defining dress. Dress as Object, Meaning and Identity. Manchester, New York 1999
Hollander, Anne: Seeing Through Clothes. New York 1979[2]
Dies.: Anzug und Eros. Eine Geschichte der modernen Kleidung. München 1997
Howell, Georgina: In Vogue. Six decades of fashion. London 1976[2]
Jedding-Gesterling, Maria und Georg **Brutscher**: Die Frisur. Eine Kulturgeschichte der Haarmode von der Antike bis zur Gegenwart. Hamburg 1988
Jones, Terry und Avril **Mair**: Fashion Now. i-D selects the world's 150 most important designers. Köln 2003
Junker, Almut und Eva **Stille**: Zur Geschichte der Unterwäsche 1700–1960. Ausst.-Kat. Historisches Museum Frankfurt. Frankfurt am Main 1988 = Kleine Schriften des Historischen Museums Frankfurt, Bd. 39
Kleider machen Leute. Kunst, Kostüme und Mode von 1700 bis 1940. Ausst.-Kat. Seedamm Kulturzentrum, Pfäffikon SZ. Lausanne 2000
Koch-Mertens, Wiebke: Der Mensch und seine Kleider. Teil I: Die Kulturgeschichte der Mode bis 1900. Düsseldorf, Zürich 2000
Koda, Harold: Extreme Beauty. The Body Transformed. Ausst.-Kat. The Metropolitan Museum of Art New York. New York 2000
König, René und Peter W. **Schuppisser**: Die Mode in der menschlichen Gesellschaft. Zürich 1958
König, René: Menschheit auf dem Laufsteg. Die Mode im Zivilisationsprozeß. München, Wien 1985
Krause, Gisela und Gertrud **Lenning**: Kleine Kostümkunde. Berlin 1995

Laver, James: Modesty in Dress. An Inquiry into the Fundamentals of Fashion. Boston 1969
Ders.: Costume & Fashion. A Concise History. London 1985
Lischka, Gerhard Johann (Hrsg.): Mode – Kult. Beiträge des Symposiums „Mode – Kult" am 7. Juli 2001 im Kornhausforum in Bern. Köln 2002
Loschek, Ingrid: Reclams Mode- und Kostümlexikon. Stuttgart 1987
Dies.: Mode. Verführung und Notwendigkeit. Struktur und Strategie der Aussehensveränderungen. München 1991
Dies.: Fashion of the Century. Chronik der Mode von 1900 bis heute. München 2001
Meij, Ietse: Haute Couture & Prêt-à-porter. Mode 1750–2000. Een Keuze uit de Kostuumcollectie Gemeentemuseum Den Haag. Bestandskatalog. Zwolle, Den Haag 1998
Milbank, Caroline Rennolds: Couture. Glanz und Geschichte der großen Modeschöpfer und ihrer Creationen. Köln 1997
Mode von Kopf bis Fuss 1750–2001. Katalog zur 273. Sonderausstellung des Historischen Museums der Stadt Wien, Hermesvilla. Wien 2001
Moments de Mode à travers les collections du Musée des Arts de la Mode. Ausst.-Kat. Musée des Arts de la Mode de Paris. Paris 1986
Mulvagh, Jane: Vogue. History of 20th Century Fashion. London 1988
Mulvey, Kate und Melissa **Richards**: Beauty & Mode. Frauenschönheit im 20. Jahrhundert. Stilempfinden, Mode, Kosmetik, Frisuren, Medien, Zeitgeschichte und Rolle der Frau in der Gesellschaft von 1890 bis 1999. Berlin 1999
Orment-Corpet, Catherine: Modes XIXe – XXe Siècles. Vicenza 2000
Reineking von Bock, Gisela: 200 Jahre Mode. Kleider vom Rokoko bis heute. Köln 1991 = Kataloge des Museums für Angewandte Kunst, Bd. XII
Ribeiro, Aileen: Dress and Morality. New York 1986
Roselle, Bruno du: La Mode. Paris 1980 = Collection Notre Siècle
Rothstein, Nathalie (Hrsg.): Four Hundred Years of Fashion. Bestandskatalog Victoria & Albert Museum. London 1984
Ruppert, Jacques, Madeleine **Delpierre**, Renée **Davray-Piékolek**, Pascale **Gorguet-Ballesteros**: Le Costume Français. Paris 2000[3] = Guides historiques. Tout l'Art Encyclopédie
Russell, Douglas A.: Costume History and Style. New Jersey 1983
Schmierer, Thomas: Modewandel und Gesellschaft. Die Dynamik von „in" und „out". Diss. München. Opladen 1995
Seeling, Charlotte: Mode. Das Jahrhundert der Designer. 1900–1999. Köln 1999
Sommer, Carlo Michael: Soziopsychologie der Kleidermode. Diss. Heidelberg 1989. Regensburg 1989 = Theorie und Forschung, Bd. 87; Psychologie, Bd. 34
Thesander, Marianne: The Feminine Ideal. London 1997
Thiel, Erika: Geschichte des Kostüms. Die europäische Mode von den Anfängen bis zur Gegenwart. Berlin 1990[5]
Vinken, Barbara: Mode nach der Mode. Kleid und Geist am Ende des 20. Jahrhunderts. Frankfurt am Main 1993
Watt, Judith: Fashion Writing. London 2000[2] = The Penguin Book of Twentieth-Century
Wiederkehr-Benz, Katrin: Sozialpsychologische Funktionen der Kleidermode. Diss. Zürich 1971. Zürich 1973
Wilcox, Claire (Hrsg.): Radical Fashion. Ausst.-Kat. Victoria & Albert Museum. London 2001

Text Bratner
Hardouin-Fugier, Elisabeth, Bernard **Berthod** und Martine **Chavent-Fusaro**: Les Etoffes. Dictionnaire historique. Paris 1994
Modes & Révolutions 1780–1804. Ausst.-Kat. Musée de la Mode et du Costume Palais Galliera. Paris 1989
Provoyeur, Pierre und Claudette **Joannis**: L'Etoffe des Héros 1789–1815. Costumes et Textiles français de la Révolution à l'Empire. Ausst.-Kat. Musée des Arts de la Mode Paris. Paris 1989
Ribeiro, Aileen: Ingres in Fashion. Representations of Dress and Appearance in Ingres's Images of Women. New Haven und London 1999
Trüber, Susanne: Mode zwischen Revolution und Restauration – Zeichnungen für das „Journal des Luxus und der Moden" (1786–1827) aus der „Sammlung Rückert". Ausst.-Kat. Städtische Sammlungen Schweinfurt. Schweinfurt 1989 = Schweinfurter Museumsschriften, Heft 29

Text Brattig
Boehn, Max von: Biedermeier. Deutschland von 1815–1847. Berlin o.J. [1923], S. 557–584
Durian-Ress, Saskia: Mode zur Zeit des Biedermeier. In: Georg **Himmelheber**: Kunst des Biedermeier. 1815–1835. Architektur, Malerei, Plastik, Kunsthandwerk, Musik, Dichtung und Mode. Ausst.-Kat. Bayerisches Nationalmuseum München. München 1988, S. 65–70 u. 268–272, Abb. 137–160

Kleinert, Annemarie: Die frühen Modejournale in Frankreich. Studien zur Literatur der Mode von den Anfängen bis 1848. Berlin 1980 = Studienreihe Romania, Bd. 5

Kosche, Thomas: Was trugen jene Badener im Biedermeier, die sich die Biedermeiermode nicht leisten konnten? Veröffentlichungsreihe „LTA-Forschung" des Landesmuseums für Technik und Arbeit in Mannheim, Heft 11/1993

Kröll, Christina: Heimliche Verführung. Ein Modejournal 1786–1827. Ausst.-Kat. Goethe-Museum Düsseldorf und Anton-und-Katharina-Kippenberg-Stiftung. Hrsg. von Jörn Göres. Düsseldorf 1978

Lehmberg, Hans: Frisuren im Biedermeier I–III. Beiblatt zu den Bildreihen. München 1968 = Institut für Film und Bild in Wissenschaft und Unterricht München

Völker, Angela: Biedermeierstoffe. Die Sammlungen des MAK – Österreichisches Museum für Angewandte Kunst, Wien und des Technischen Museums Wien. München, New York 1996

Waidenschlager, Christine: Die Mode zwischen Biedermeier und Gründerzeit. In: **Dies.** (Hrsg.): Berliner Chic. Mode von 1820 bis 1990. Ausst.-Kat. Stiftung Stadtmuseum Berlin. Berlin 2001, S. 34–67

Weber-Kellermann, Ingeborg: Frauenleben im 19. Jahrhundert. Empire und Romantik, Biedermeier, Gründerzeit. München 1983

Wendel, Friedrich: Die Mode in der Karikatur. Dresden 1928

Text Ellwanger

Douglas, Mary: Ritual, Tabu und Körpersymbolik. Sozialanthropologische Studien in Industriegesellschaft und Stammeskultur. Frankfurt am Main 1981

Ellwanger, Karen: Bekleidung im Modernisierungsprozeß. Frauen, Mode, Mobilität. Diss. Dortmund 1994

Lethen, Helmut: Verhaltenslehren der Kälte. Lebensversuche zwischen den Kriegen. Frankfurt am Main 1994

Martin, Emily: Die neue Kultur der Gesundheit. Soziale Geschlechtsidentität und das Immunsystem in Amerika. In: **Sarasin**, Philip und Jakob **Tanner** (Hrsg.): Physiologie und industrielle Gesellschaft. Frankfurt am Main 1998, S. 508–525

Perrot, Philippe: Fashioning the Bourgeoisie. London, New York 1994

Reznicek, Paula von: Die Auferstehung der Dame. Stuttgart 1928

Sennett, Richard: Verfall und Ende des öffentlichen Lebens. Die Tyrannei der Intimität. Frankfurt am Main 1986

Stepanowa, Warwara: Die heutige Kleidung. Die ‚Prozodeschda'. In: **Stern**, Radu (Hrsg.): Gegen den Strich. A contre-courant. Kleider von Künstlern 1900 bis 1940. Ausst.-Kat. Bern 1992, S. 192–130

Text Gaugele

Burchard, Doris: Der Kampf um die Schönheit. Jahrhundertkarrieren. Helena Rubinstein, Elizabeth Arden, Estee Lauder. München 1998

Featherstone, Mike: The Body in Consumer Culture. In: Theory, Culture & Society, Bd. 1, o.O. 1982, S. 18–33

Lahmann, Heinrich: Die Reform der Kleidung. Stuttgart 1898

Mohrbutter, Alfred: Das Kleid der Frau. Darmstadt, Leipzig 1904

Muthesius, Anna: Das Eigenkleid der Frau. Krefeld 1903

Pudor, Heinrich: Die Frauenreformkleidung. Ein Beitrag zu Philosophie, Hygiene und Ästhetik des Kleides. Leipzig 1903

Schultze-Naumburg, Paul: Die Kultur des weiblichen Körpers als Grundlage der Frauenkleidung. Jena 1910

Stamm, Brigitte: Auf dem Weg zum Reformkleid. Die Kritik des Korsetts und der diktierten Mode. In: **Siepmann**, Eckard (Hrsg.): Kunst und Alltag um 1900. 3. Jahrbuch des Werkbund-Archivs. Gießen 1978, S. 117–178

Sykora, Katharina: Weibliche Kunst-Körper zwischen Bildersturm und Erlösungspathos. In: **Welsch**, Wolfgang: Die Aktualität des Ästhetischen. München 1993, S. 94–115

Van de Velde, Henry: Die künstlerische Hebung der Frauentracht. Krefeld 1900

Van de Velde, Maria: Einleitung zum Album moderner, nach Künstlerentwürfen ausgeführter Damenkleider, ausgestellt auf der großen allgemeinen Ausstellung für das Bekleidungswesen, Krefeld 1900, Düsseldorf 1900

Wunderle, Michaela: Apropos Helena Rubinstein. Frankfurt am Main 1995

Impressum / Imprint

© 2003 ARNOLDSCHE Art Publishers, Stuttgart, Museum für Angewandte Kunst Köln und die Autoren / and the authors
© 2003 der abgebildeten Werke und Fotografien bei den Künstlern, Fotografen, Models, Agenturen und Instituten / for the works and photographs shown by the artists, photographers, models, agencies and institutes

Alle Rechte vorbehalten. Vervielfältigung und Wiedergabe auf jegliche Weise (grafisch, elektronisch und fotomechanisch sowie der Gebrauch von Systemen zur Datenrückgewinnung) – auch in Auszügen – nur mit schriftlicher Genehmigung der ARNOLDSCHEN Verlagsanstalt GmbH, Liststraße 9, D–70180 Stuttgart und des Museums für Angewandte Kunst Köln.
All rights reserved. No part of this work may be reproduced or used in any forms or by any means (graphic, electronic or mechanical, including photocopying or information storage and retrieval systems) without written permission from the copyright holder.

Herausgeber / General Editor
Patricia Brattig
Museum für Angewandte Kunst Köln / Museum of Applied Art Cologne

Idee, Konzeption und Projektleitung / Idea, conception and project head
Patricia Brattig

Kuratorin historische Mode / Curator historical fashion
Patricia Brattig

Gastkuratorin moderne und zeitgenössische Mode / Guest curator modern and contemporary fashion
Eva Gronbach, Köln

Redaktion / Editors
Luzie Bratner, Patricia Brattig

Grafische Gestaltung / Layout
Kristine Klein, Köln

Fotografien (Neuaufnahmen der Museumskostüme) / Costume photography
Anna C. Wagner, Rheinisches Bildarchiv, Köln / Cologne
assistiert von / assisted by
Nicole Cronauge

Reproduktionen / Repros
Rolf Zimmermann, Rheinisches Bildarchiv, Köln

Scherenschnitte (als Outlines) / Silhouettes (outlines)
Akiko Bernhöft, Köln

Outlines der Catwalk-Abbildungen / Catwalk outlines
Kristine Klein, Köln

Offset-Reproduktionen / Offset Reproductions
Repromayer, Reutlingen

Druck / Printed by
Rung-Druck, Göppingen

Dieses Buch wurde gedruckt auf 100% chlorfrei gebleichtem Papier und entspricht damit dem TCF-Standard.
This book has been printed on paper that is 100% free of chlorine bleach in conformity with TCF standards.

Bibliographische Information Der Deutschen Bibliothek
Die Deutsche Bibliothek verzeichnet diese Publikation in der Deutschen Nationalbibliografie; detaillierte bibliografische Daten sind im Internet über **http://dnb.ddb.de** abrufbar.
Bibliographical information: Die Deutsche Bibliothek
Die Deutsche Bibliothek lists this publication in the Deutsche Nationalbibliografie; detailed bibliographical data are available on the Internet at **http://dnb.ddb.de**

ISBN 3-89790-215-X
Made in Germany, 2003

Die Publikation erscheint anlässlich der Ausstellung „**in.** femme fashion 1780–2004. Die Modellierung des Weiblichen in der Mode"
Published to accompany the exhibition „**in.** femme fashion 1780–2004. The Modelling of the Female Form in Fashion"
Museum für Angewandte Kunst Köln, An der Rechtschule, D-50667 Köln
19. Oktober 2003 bis 14. Dezember 2003

Leihgeber / Loan collection

Walter van Beirendonck, Antwerpen
Bless, Paris/Berlin
Bühnen der Stadt Köln
Hussein Chalayan, London
CHANEL, Paris
Christian Dior Archives, Paris
Elternhaus® Maegde u. Knechte®, Hamburg
Katharina Evers, Köln
Jean Paul Gaultier SA, Paris
Romeo Gigli, Mailand
Thomas Grünfeld, Köln
goyagoya, Darmstadt
Eva Gronbach, Köln
Heimat, Andreas Hoyer und Andy Scherpereel, Köln
Hermès, Paris
Ja!-Jungs, Offenbach
Kölnisches Stadtmuseum
Stephen Jones, London
Lutz, Paris
Maison Martin Margiela, Paris
Thierry Mugler, Paris
Barbara Ott, Düsseldorf
Dieter Pool, Köln
Darja Richter, Paris
Stephan Schneider, Antwerpen
Heather Sheehan, Köln
Strenesse Gabriele Strehle, Nördlingen
A.F. Vandevorst, Antwerpen